THE
CORETTA
SCOTT KING
AWARDS

*ALA Editions purchases fund advocacy,
awareness, and accreditation programs for
library professionals worldwide.*

THE CORETTA SCOTT KING AWARDS

SIXTH EDITION

Edited by
CAROLE J. McCOLLOUGH *and*
ADELAIDE PONIATOWSKI PHELPS

The Coretta Scott King Book Awards Committee
Ethnic and Multicultural Information Exchange Round Table

CHICAGO 2019

CAROLE J. McCOLLOUGH, PhD, is a retired associate professor of library science from Wayne State University in Detroit. She is a past chair of the Coretta Scott King Task Force as well as a past chair of the Coretta Scott King Book Award Jury. She is a current board member of the Children's Defense Fund's Langston Hughes Library and of the Southfield (Michigan) Public Library.

ADELAIDE PONIATOWSKI PHELPS has a master's degree in library and information science from Wayne State University in Detroit and a second master's degree in English literature from Oakland University in Rochester, Michigan. She is a past coordinator of the Educational Resources Lab in the School of Education and Human Services at Oakland University and a past lecturer in children's literature for the reading department. In addition, she served two terms on the Coretta Scott King Book Award Jury (2007–2008).

Adelaide and Carole co-edited the fifth edition of the *Coretta Scott King Awards 1970–2014* and co-authored *Coretta Scott King Award Books Discussion Guide: Pathways to Democracy* (American Library Association, 2014).

© 2019 by the American Library Association

Extensive effort has gone into ensuring the reliability of the information in this book; however, the publisher makes no warranty, express or implied, with respect to the material contained herein.

ISBN: 978-0-8389-1869-2 (paper)

Library of Congress Cataloging-in-Publication Data

Names: McCollough, Carole J., editor. | Phelps, Adelaide Poniatowski, editor. |
    Ethnic and Multicultural Information Exchange Round Table. Coretta Scott King Book
    Awards Committee.
Title: The Coretta Scott King awards : 50th anniversary / edited by Carole J. McCollough and
    Adelaide Poniatowski Phelps.
Description: Sixth edition. | Chicago : ALA Editions, 2019. | "The Coretta Scott King Book
    Awards Committee, Ethnic and Multicultural Information Exchange Round Table." | Includes
    bibliographical references and index.
Identifiers: LCCN 2019010142 | ISBN 9780838918692 (paper : alk. paper)
Subjects: LCSH: Coretta Scott King Award. | American literature—African American authors—
    Bibliography. | American literature—African American authors—Awards. | Children's
    literature, American—Bibliography. | Children's literature, American—Awards. | African
    Americans in literature—Bibliography. | Children—Books and reading—United States.
Classification: LCC Z1037.A2 C67 2019 | DDC 016.8108/0928208996073—dc23
LC record available at https://lccn.loc.gov/2019010142

Book design by Kimberly Thornton in the Chaparral and Brandon Grotesque typefaces.
Cover background © kastanka/Adobe Stock; dove © KatyaKatya/Adobe Stock.

♾ This paper meets the requirements of ANSI/NISO Z39.48–1992 (Permanence of Paper).

Printed in the United States of America

23 22 21 20 19   5 4 3 2 1

Dedicated to
Henrietta M. Smith

CONTENTS

FOREWORD

It's a celebration! A celebration of a remarkable and historic journey to this momentous milestone. The entire year of 2019 marks the celebration of the fiftieth anniversary of the Coretta Scott King (CSK) Book Awards. The Coretta Scott King Book Awards have enlarged the prominence of literature for children and youth about the Black experience and has heightened the work of our author and illustrator winners and honorees. The support of the awards by people of all backgrounds and around the world has been unwavering and has empowered the Coretta Scott King Book Awards to endure for 50 years and beyond.

The Coretta Scott King Book Award has become one of the most prestigious citations in children's literature. It continues to recognize outstanding African American authors and artists of children's books who demonstrate an appreciation of Black culture and universal values. The distinguished works and contributions of the author and illustrator winners and honorees are in this 6th edition, 50th anniversary, publication. See, read, share, and enjoy!

Dr. Claudette S. McLinn
Chair, Coretta Scott King Book Awards Committee
Ethnic and Multicultural Information Exchange Round Table
American Library Association

ACKNOWLEDGMENTS

We gratefully acknowledge Oakland University's Educational Resources Lab (ERL) for providing space for research and access to their collections. An extra word of thanks to Jamie Santoro, acquisitions editor, ALA Editions, for her conference calls of support that kept us on track. In addition, Adelaide would like to acknowledge her husband, Tom, for his understanding of the time commitment required and recognition of the value of the work that the CSK committee does. In addition, Carole and Adelaide would like to thank Tom for providing them with an abundance of chocolate to keep up their energy. Carole would like to acknowledge her great-granddaughter, Rhylan, as a living example of the value of seeing herself in books about the Black experience. Most importantly we are indebted to Henrietta M. Smith for providing the framework and setting the standards that enabled us to complete this 50th anniversary edition.

HISTORY OF
THE AWARD

The Coretta Scott King Book Award and its association with the American Library Association (ALA) originated in 1969. It came as the result of a discussion between two librarians, Glyndon Flynt Greer and Mabel McKissick, and the publisher John Carroll. The impetus flowed from the observation that no African American author or illustrator had ever been honored by the prestigious Newbery and Caldecott awards, established in 1922 and 1938, respectively, and sponsored by what was then the ALA Children's Service Division. It was thought that the establishment of a special award would bring attention to the fine work produced by African American authors and illustrators in books for children and young people. The first award was presented during the New Jersey Library Association meeting in May 1970. The first winner was the late Lillie Patterson, who was honored for her young readers' edition of the life of Martin Luther King Jr., written shortly after his assassination. Over the next twelve years, without official recognition from the executive board of ALA, the presentations continued, and in 1974 an illustrator award category was added. The first to receive that award was George Ford, for the illustrations in Sharon Mathis's biography *Ray Charles*.

In 1982, through the efforts of E. J. Josey, an ALA councilor, the awards committee, chaired by Effie Lee Morris, was named the Coretta Scott King Task Force and became a part of the ALA Social Responsibilities Round Table

(SRRT). This congenial union remained in place until the ALA midwinter meeting in January 2004 in San Diego. Under the leadership of chairperson Fran Ware and past chairs Carole J. McCollough and Barbara Jones Clark, the task force's affiliation was changed from the Social Responsibilities Round Table to the Ethnic and Multicultural Information Exchange Round Table (EMIERT)—the rationale being that the goals and missions of the task force were more closely aligned with those of EMIERT. All was done with the approval and blessings of the action council of SRRT. The Coretta Scott King Task Force expressed appreciation to SRRT for its twenty-four years of working together.

In a continuous process of growth and visionary expansion, the task force functions under well-constructed bylaws. Included in this organizational pattern is the clear definition of the makeup, length of terms, and responsibilities of the seven-member awards jury. Also included are established criteria for the selection of the award-winning titles:

Thematically, the material (text or illustration) must speak to some aspect of African American culture, with an awareness of Martin Luther King Jr.'s sense of the brotherhood of all cultures.

- The author or illustrator must be African American.
- The content (illustration or text) must be of high literary or visual quality, with a theme that has the potential for long-term, meaningful significance.
- Only books published the year preceding a jury's period of deliberation are eligible for consideration.
- Books must be published in the United States.
- The winner of the Coretta Scott King/John Steptoe New Talent Award must meet the same standards as winners of the other awards, but eligibility is limited to works of those who have had no more than three books published.

Since 1972, the awards have been presented at a gala breakfast. The breakfast, held during the ALA annual conference, is marked by ever-increasing attendance. Each winner in art and text receives an honorarium, the value of which continues to grow. The honorarium for the winners has been a gift from the Johnson Publishing Company since the award's inception in 1970. The winners also receive a plaque and a set of encyclopedias, one from Encyclopedia Britannica and the other from World Book, Inc. In keeping with the times, the encyclopedias are now on discs. In 1995, the first Genesis Award for new talent was presented. This award, which was later officially renamed the Coretta Scott King/John Steptoe New Talent Award, recognizes a writer or illustrator whose early potential speaks of things to come. The first recipient, Sharon M. Draper, the author of *Tears of a Tiger*, went on to become a Coretta Scott King award winner in 1998 for her novel *Forged by Fire*. She continues to be recognized not only for novels about contemporary young adults (*November Blues* received a Coretta Scott King author honor in 2008) but also for her monumental, thoroughly researched historical novel *Copper Sun*, which won the Coretta Scott King author award in 2007.

Since 1984, among the special highlights at each breakfast is the presence of children, the ones to whom the books are designed to speak. These young guests, sponsored by generous donors, come from the geographical area of ALA's annual conference. For some of the young people attending the breakfast, there is a moment of special individual recognition. Each year, starting in 1999, Disney/Jump at the Sun has sponsored an essay contest for students who live in the area of the conference. From papers written by elementary and middle school students, judges choose the best paper about a preselected book. The audience is always delighted with the poise with which the young winners read their essays and graciously thank the award sponsors and the Coretta Scott King Book Awards Committee for their special opportunity and the scholarship check. Other support comes from the publishing houses of the winning titles. Each young guest goes home with a selection from the winning and honor books for his/her personal collection. The publishers further collaborate on the design and production of the study guides created by each awards jury. The guides are distributed at the breakfast and are available through the ALA Office of Library Outreach Services (OLOS) as long as the supply lasts.

As the Coretta Scott King Book Awards Committee looked forward to the commemoration of its fortieth anniversary, the members celebrated, in 2009, the life of its last surviving founder, Mabel McKissick, after twenty-seven years as a school librarian in Connecticut and elsewhere. 2009 was also the time to remember the late Basil Phillips, photographic editor for *Ebony* magazine. Phillips was instrumental in establishing the author honorarium through the largesse of John Johnson, founder of Johnson Publishing. The memory of our stalwart leaders will be a permanent part of the Coretta Scott King Book Awards history.

Coretta Scott King award-winning books can be recognized by a seal designed in 1974 by the internationally known artist Lev Mills, who at the time was artist-in-residence at Atlanta University. The elements of this official seal convey the principles to which Martin Luther King Jr. was dedicated. Within a circle, which represents continuity, sits a child reading a book. The five religious symbols below the image of the child represent non-sectarianism: star and crescent (Islam), om (Hinduism), cross (Christianity), Star of David (Judaism), and yin-yang (Taoism). The seal also includes a dove of peace and a superimposed pyramid, a tribute to human strength and to the strength of Atlanta University, where the award was headquartered at the time the seal was designed.

The original seals for the winners were printed in bronze, which represented the earth tones of Mother Africa, and the seals for the honor books were printed in tones of silver. In the late 1990s, without a change in the design, the seals were produced in a more environmentally friendly format—a black background with character details superimposed in bronze for winners and in pewter for honor books. The seal for the Coretta Scott King/John Steptoe New Talent Award is detailed in green, a color symbolic of new beginnings.

Among the many highlights in the history of the Coretta Scott King Book Awards are Legends, Folklore, and Real Life Stories: The Coretta Scott King Award Books, a special exhibit of illustrations from award winners mounted by the Art Institute of Chicago from July 2000 to February 2001. In addition, educational programs and workshops were conducted by some of the illustrators whose works were on display.

During the tenure of chair Barbara Jones Clark, the task force launched a national awareness campaign to acquaint a wider audience with the role the Coretta Scott King Book Awards play in showcasing the valuable and informative works of African American authors and illustrators. The late Virginia Hamilton served as honorary chairperson of the committee that spearheaded this endeavor in 1998. In 2008–2009, chair Deborah Taylor, working with author and editor Andrea Pinkney, widened the visibility of the Coretta Scott King Book Awards by launching a broad-based Fortieth Anniversary Public Awareness Program, which showcased a handsome broadside by award-winning artist Kadir Nelson and a celebratory poem by Arnold Adoff.

The first edition of *The Coretta Scott King Awards* was published in 1994. It presented the history of the award, biographical sketches of winners and honor recipients, annotations of each title, and handsome reproductions of illustrations from award winners published from 1974 to 1994. Following the same format, the second edition was published in 1999, the third edition in 2004, the fourth edition in 2009, the fifth edition in 2014, and now the sixth edition in 2019. Each new edition is updated to make the material more relevant and more useful to a wider audience. With an attitude of always looking forward and broadening the vision of the Coretta Scott King Book Awards Committee, in 2010 a new award category was added. In appreciation and remembrance of the late Virginia Hamilton, the Coretta Scott King–Virginia Hamilton Award for Lifetime Achievement was established. Over each three-year cycle, an author, illustrator, and librarian in the field will be recognized for their body of work. Each recipient will receive an honorarium, a medal emblazoned with his/her name, and a photograph of the late "word master" Virginia Hamilton. The first recipients were author Walter Dean Myers, illustrator Ashley Bryan, and librarian Henrietta M. Smith.

The Coretta Scott King Book Awards Committee is indebted to Henrietta M. Smith for her many contributions, including as editor of the first four editions of *The Coretta Scott King Awards* and as author of the history.

AUTHOR AWARDS
1970–2019

2019 WINNER

HARTFIELD, CLAIRE. *A Few Red Drops: The Chicago Race Riot of 1919.* Clarion Books, 2018. Gr. 5–8*

A Few Red Drops is a well-researched exposé of the Black experience during a slice in time, albeit a dark time for American history, in 1919. Claire Hartfield is an excellent story-teller who weaves in and out of the events surrounding the infamous race riots in July 1919 and the tensions, people, places, and things that gave rise to it. The book serves to anchor this time and place in history as being a pivotal point for Blacks who were trying to carve out an existence in what was thought at the time to be a land of milk and honey. A clear, well-written text, and detailed back matter, include photographs and a map of the racial divide in Chicago neighborhoods in 1919. Hartfield connects readers to a seminal period in our country's history. *A Few Red Drops* shines as a teaching tool and a solid addition to any unit on civil, labor, or human rights and the Great Migration. —*Jason Driver*

2019 HONORS

CLINE-RANSOME, LESA. *Finding Langston.* Holiday House, 2018. Gr. 3–7

A true gem, *Finding Langston* is an elegant and deceptively simple read that examines the life of a boy trying to find his place in the world following the death of his mother. Langston, named for Langston Hughes, and his father move from a sleepy southern town to bustling 1946 Chicago. This book has richly developed characters and a clear sense of setting in Bronzeville, Chicago, during the Great Migration. After finding the poetry of Langston Hughes at the local library, eleven-year-old Langston grows and changes while uncovering the richness of the written word. This book encourages self-examination through the lens of Langston during a time of transformation and renaissance around issues of race, identity, culture, and education that closely resemble today's reality for African Americans in Chicago and the United States. —*LaKeshia Darden*

JOHNSON, VARIAN. *The Parker Inheritance.* Arthur A. Levine Books: an imprint of Scholastic Inc., 2018. Gr. 4–8.

This compelling and suspenseful story weaves a multigenerational mystery that draws from history but remains in the present. With wit and candor, this middle-grade novel refuses to shy away from racism and inequity. Candice and her mother relocate to her grandmother's home in a small town in South Carolina. When Candice finds a strange letter and bracelet in the attic, she wonders if they may point to her grandmother's strange actions from the past. While Candice and her friend Brandon look for clues in contemporary South Carolina, flashbacks tell the story of the Washington family, revealing truths about the town's racist history and showing the complexity of the African American experience. A well-crafted mystery that informs as much as it entertains, this adventurous novel weaves rich historical facts with current race and gender discourse to leave the reader thinking about the book's themes long after finishing. —*Christina Vortia*

MAGOON, KEKLA. *The Season of Styx Malone.* Wendy Lamb Books, an imprint of Random House Children's Books, a division of Penguin Random House LLC, New York, 2018. Gr. 4–7.

Magoon gives readers a poignant tale about the importance of the African American family. This coming-of-age story centers around two brothers living in rural Indiana, safely protected by their parents, but eager to experience adventure. Their father wants to protect his family from the supposed dangers of the urban environment. Trouble arises when his sons become friends with an older boy who is new to the neighborhood. The author expands themes of love for family and friends, adoption, and foster care. This book feels like a throwback—the folksy front cover doesn't lie about what you're going to get when you read *Styx Malone*—and yet it is rooted in contemporary issues. With strong, well-developed characters interspersed with touches of humor, Styx Malone demonstrates the challenges of raising Black boys to adulthood in the United States and acknowledges the importance of the community in helping those who are less fortunate. —*Sam Bloom*

2019 JOHN STEPTOE NEW TALENT AWARD

JACKSON, TIFFANY D. *Monday's Not Coming.* Katherine Tegen Books, an imprint of HarperCollins Publishers, 2018. Gr. 7–12.

Monday's Not Coming is a powerful young adult novel about the disappearance of Monday, a girl from southeast Washington, D.C. A strong narrative voice and propulsive plot clearly outline the angst that Claudia feels as she struggles to piece together the story of what happened to her best friend, Monday. In alternating chapters that explore and reveal pieces of the girls' friendship and events that happened before and after Monday's disappearance, readers must piece together the fragmented story while deciding if Claudia is a reliable narrator. This timely thriller was inspired by the disappearance of Black girls in Washington, D.C., and it features a mind-blowing resolution. Jackson's skillfully told tale examines friendship, child abuse, and family relationships, and it explores what happens when society turns a blind eye to kids who fall through the cracks. —*LaKeshia Darden*

2018 WINNER

WATSON, RENÉE. *Piecing Me Together.*
Bloomsbury, 2017. Gr. 6–12.

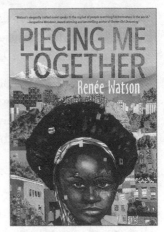

Jade is a collage artist, a high school junior, and an African American female who often feels fragmented. Is she the scholarship student at her wealthy, almost all-white school? Is she Max's "mentee" in the Women to Women program? Is "a black girl's life . . . only about being stitched together and coming undone?"

As Jade broadens her horizons through the mentorship program, she also realizes that what her "small" world has to offer is infinite. Her growing sense of self and her community enables Jade to educate her teachers, her mentors, her classmates, and her friends. Watson shows every piece of Jade, every internal and external conflict, every bit of beauty, intelligence, fear, bravery, and strength. While *Piecing Me Together* looks head-on at white privilege, institutional racism, and police brutality, it also focuses on how magical and transformative art and community can be. —*Sharon Levin*

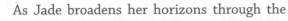

2018 HONORS

REYNOLDS, JASON. *Long Way Down.* Simon & Schuster, 2017. Gr. 6–12.

Long Way Down introduces Jason Reynolds's readers to a previously unseen facet of this young author's talent. Fifteen-year-old Will hears the shots, and

> ran,
> ducked,
> hid,
> tucked . . .
> pressed our lips to the
> pavement and prayed (p. 10).

Will waited to count the bodies, but there was only one—his brother Shawn's. He hears the sirens' wail; he hears Shawn girlfriend's screams; he hears his mother's sobs that continue forever. There are neighborhood rules he must follow: no crying, no snitching, revenge. Although he has never touched a gun, Will knows where Shawn's is hidden. He cannot allow his brother's murder to go unavenged.

This magical realism novel in verse moves from Will's eighth-floor apartment on an excruciating elevator journey to the building's entrance. From floor to floor, the door slides open for the ghost of a murdered man—father, grandfather, uncle, brother—who recreates his own murder. Reynolds's poetic allusions and recurring images will keep readers wide-eyed through to the jolting shock on the final page. —*Linda M. Pavonetti*

THOMAS, ANGIE. *The Hate U Give*. Balzer & Bray HarperCollins, 2017. Gr. 9–12.

Sixteen-year-old Starr is the sole witness to her friend Khalil's fatal shooting by a police officer. Overwhelmed, Starr must testify before a grand jury while questioning her role in speaking out in Khalil's memory. *The Hate U Give* brilliantly sheds light on this tragedy by humanizing the participants. Starr has mastered living in two worlds. She attends a private, majority-white school while living in a crime-ridden neighborhood. Dealing with the aftermath of the shooting causes her to question everything she once thought she understood. Thomas's novel never insults the reader with easy answers. Rather, it is filled with realistic characters, authentic and nuanced dialogue, and situations for which there are no easy answers. While the Black Lives Matter movement inspired the novel, *The Hate U Give* isn't about a movement. It's about Black lives living, loving, pursuing happiness, and deserving freedom—just like everyone else. —*Kathy Caroll*

BARNES, DERRICK. *Crown: An Ode to the Fresh Cut*. Illustrated by Gordon C. James. Bolden Books/Agate Publishing, 2017. Gr. Pre-K–12.

The pride of being a princely African American male spans this book through diverse images of brilliant, majestic Black men. The author and illustrator weave in the power of Black male identities through fluid and inspirational illustrations and poetic voice.

The reader appreciates the diversity of Blackness by engaging in the barbershop experience through the joy visible on beautifully authentic faces: "They're going to have to wear shades/when they look up to catch your shine." The iconic socio-political cultural significance of the brotherhood of a Black barbershop draws the reader into a visit that is always more than just a haircut. It is a statement, an affirmation, and a shout-out to the potential that exists within this community of men.

Crown's message resonates with a powerful lesson of pride eliminating stereotypical images by depicting diverse Black features: noses, lips, cheekbones, and hair. This book sends a clear message that African American males leave the barbershop with an emboldened swagger, a new haircut, and the realization that there are no limits to who they can become. —*Omobolade Delano-Oriarian, Suzanne Fondrie, and Marguerite W. Penick-Parks*

2018 JOHN STEPTOE NEW TALENT AWARD

MOORE, DAVID BARCLAY. *The Stars Beneath Our Feet.* Knopf, 2017. Gr. 5–8.

Twelve-year-old Wallace "Lolly" Rachpaul is still reeling from the gang-related murder of his older brother Jermaine. When Lolly receives a large bag of Legos from his mother's girlfriend, he begins to create an imaginary city that outgrows his room. Mr. Ali, director of the rec center, offers Lolly the use of a vacant storage area for his creation. When Mr. Ali allows Big Rose, another loner, to build in the area as well, Lolly is perturbed. Over time, he and Rose bond over their creations. The bridge between Lolly's imaginary city and Rose's very detailed rendition of the St. Nick projects becomes a gathering point for the whole community. Lolly's journey through grief is a tough one. His father seems unavailable most of the time, but in the end he comes through for Lolly. When his best friend Vega is tempted by his cousin's crew to commit an act of vengeance, Lolly has to make a tough choice of whether or not to join him. In the end, it is the greater community that rallies around Lolly when he needs it most. And it is at this point that Lolly sees himself as Wallace with hope for a better future. —*Bina Williams*

2017 WINNER

LEWIS, JOHN, AND ANDREW AYDIN. *March: Book Three.* Illustrated by Nate Powell. Top Shelf Productions, 2016. Gr. 6–9*

March: Book Three is a firsthand account of the Civil Rights Movement through Lewis's eyes. Using vivid language and dynamic storytelling, it details events from Freedom Summer to the 1965 Voting Rights

Act. Readers experience the realities of segregation, the sacrifices required for the struggle and the courage that defines true leaders. —*Ida Thompson*

2017 HONORS

REYNOLDS, JASON. *As Brave as You.* Atheneum, 2016. Gr. 4–8.

Eleven-year-old Genie and fourteen-year-old Ernie demonstrate the personality twists and turns that brothers often display. It is easy to tell them apart. Genie has a notebook full of questions that he often Googles. Ernie wears dark glasses that make him appear the epitome of sophistication. While their mom and dad go to Jamaica to fix a shaky marriage, Genie and Ernie stay in North Hill, Virginia, with their grandparents.

The grandparents come with their own quirks and twists. Grandma has a list of rules that she expects them to follow. Grandpop is a mystery, and Genie watches him closely. Grandpop wears dark glasses—not to be "cool" but to hide his blindness. He carries a pistol tucked in the waistband of his pants and visits a secret room full of birds. Ernie gets a girlfriend whose father has a most unusual arrangement with Grandpop. By the time Genie and Ernie's parents arrive back in North Hill to pick up the boys, they have experienced an unforgettable, four-week rite of passage. This is a contemporary story that young readers will enjoy. —*Barbara Spears*

BRYAN, ASHLEY. *Freedom Over Me: Eleven Slaves, Their Lives and Dreams Brought to Life by Ashley Bryan.* Atheneum, 2016. Gr. 4–6.

Garnering both a CSK Author Honor and an Illustrator Honor, Ashley Bryan has created a finely crafted piece of historical fiction through free-verse poetry. The Fairfield Estates appraisement document inspired the stories of eleven slaves sold from the same plantation in 1828. For each slave, Bryan juxtaposes poems and collaged illustrations—one stark reality, and the other full-color dreams for what life could be. The poems lend a distinct voice for each character. The book concludes with the appraisement reproduced beside a typed version and an author's note explaining the history behind the documents. It is a complete package—from the chain link on the cover that binds the eleven to the back cover of the Fairchild Big House. —*Christina Dorr*

2017 JOHN STEPTOE NEW TALENT AWARD

YOON, NICOLA. *The Sun Is Also a Star*. Delacorte Press, 2016. Gr. 6–12.

Fate leads to love for Jamaican-American teen Natasha, who is fighting deportation. As her battle to remain in the United States begins, Natasha meets Daniel—a Korean-American who despises his overachieving brother. Daniel is torn between his chosen career path and poetry, where his heart lies. Natasha and Daniel are two high school students trying to identify their place in the cosmos. Finding comfort in each other's presence, Natasha and Daniel spend the next twelve hours hoping the universe has a future for their relationship. *The Sun Is Also a Star* is strikingly out of the ordinary. Yoon's dexterous writing creates an intricately woven novel, including themes of diversity, immigration, first love, and social and family issues. —*Erica Marks*

2016 WINNER

WILLIAMS-GARCIA, RITA. *Gone Crazy in Alabama*. Amistad/HarperCollins, 2015. Gr. 5–8.

Williams-Garcia paints a vivid picture of a loving family in her emotion-packed book, *Gone Crazy in Alabama*. Although it is the third in a trilogy, this book works well as a stand-alone. Williams-Garcia tells the story of three sisters traveling to Alabama to visit family. The advice that the girls are given as they travel will still resonate with children and teens of today. The three viewpoints of the sisters bring various perspectives to the reader, making the book accessible. The relationship between the great-grandmothers and the use of their stories provide even deeper insight into the family and its history. Powerful storytelling and vernacular language make this a book that tugs at readers' heartstrings. As strained relationships heal, powerful characters and emotional writing leave readers feeling deeply satisfied. —*April Roy*

2016 HONORS

REYNOLDS, JASON, AND BRENDAN KIELY. *All American Boys.* Atheneum, 2015. Gr. 7–12.

It's Friday, and Rashad is looking forward to the weekend with friends, but he makes a quick stop at the corner bodega for chips and gum. A series of unlikely events, however, leads to him being handcuffed, badly beaten, charged, and hospitalized. Tensions in his family, school, and community escalate and shine a light on police and social injustice.

Told in alternating narratives, Rashad, who is Black, and Quinn, who is white, expose the complications of confronting prejudice, racial profiling, and police brutality. Rashad's fight to prove his innocence and Quinn's dilemma in coming forth with crucial information about the incident, socially tagged by his friends as *#Rashad Is Absent Again Today,* polarize and energize the community.

The characters are authentic and convincing, the situations that entangle their lives are genuine, and the implications of everyone's decisions are long lasting. The authors' intentional challenge to the stereotype of what "all American" means is a clever title and storyline, solidifying this story's role in the social consciousness of our country. Reynolds and Kiely have created a masterpiece. —*Ida W. Thompson*

REYNOLDS, JASON. *The Boy in the Black Suit.* Atheneum, 2015. Gr. 7–10.

Matt's mother dies, he has lost his senior work-study job, his father has reverted to drinking, and he is now responsible for his family's stability. Everything that was stable and secure is suddenly in turmoil. Matt is unable to move forward until he meets Lovey, who works at the local Cluck Bucket restaurant. Matt's mourning and isolation are upended by Lovey, who is his complete opposite—self-confident, determined, and tough.

Matt begins to wear a black suit every day, the perfect attire for his new job at the local funeral home. He sits quietly at many of the funerals, watching the mourners cry and express their grief, which in a strange way helps him cope with his loss. Matt's quiet determination and venture into a romantic friendship balance the hardships of his life with the prospects of an expectant future.

Jason Reynolds's realistic characters and authentic writing are masterful, commanding the readers' attention from start to finish. This is a powerful story of loss and discovery that is genuinely and superbly told. —*Ida W. Thompson*

SHABAZZ, ILYASAH, WITH KEKLA MAGOON. *X—A Novel.* Candlewick Press, 2015. Gr. 9–12.

The early and formative years of Malcolm X are clearly detailed in this rich and gritty book written by one of his daughters. The honest language, imagery, metaphor, and introspective language take older readers on an insightful journey from Michigan to Boston and through Harlem in the 1940s. Though this book is a work of fiction, it offers a great deal of insight into the experiences that formed the complexities of this powerful civil rights leader. A timeline of Malcolm's life, and his family tree, are included along with a bibliography. —*April Roy*

2016 JOHN STEPTOE NEW TALENT AWARD

SMITH, RONALD L. *Hoodoo.* Houghton Mifflin Harcourt, 2015. Gr. 5–7.

Hoodoo Hatcher is a twelve-year-old boy who's never shown a lick of magical ability. Despite his name, he doesn't have any hoodoo in him, unlike everyone else in his family. And then a foreboding Stranger comes to Hoodoo's small Alabama town searching for a boy named Hoodoo. But why? And how can Hoodoo stop the Stranger if he doesn't have any magic of his own? Smith's multi-layered narrative is heavy with southern gothic atmosphere and boasts a dynamic first-person voice. Hoodoo's account of his experiences in a small Alabama town in the 1930s is fully realized, so richly drawn it feels as if the reader could step into the world on the page. And Smith seems to innately understand how to dial up the scary just enough to give young readers the shivers. This is a deliciously creepy debut. —*Sam Bloom*

WEATHERFORD, CAROLE BOSTON. *Voice of Freedom: Fannie Lou Hamer— Spirit of the Civil Rights Movement.* Illustrated by Ekua Holmes. Candlewick Press, 2015. Gr. 5–7*

Veteran biographer Weatherford uses free verse to tell the story of pioneering civil rights hero Fannie Lou Hamer. "All my life I've been sick and tired," Hamer famously said. "Now I'm sick and tired of being sick and tired."

Weatherford's poems reveal Hamer's strength, courage, and determination. Newcomer Holmes's collage illustrations beautifully extend Weatherford's verse. The art brilliantly establishes mood, from the ghostly bags of cotton on the backs of sharecroppers to the unflinching "Delta Blues" to the doves (or dove-shaped blossoms) on the leaves hanging over Hamer and her daughters. Holmes also brilliantly captures the subject's humanity in her art. The newsprint, tissue paper, and map of Mississippi that Holmes melds together create the portrait of Pap and Fannie Lou opposite "Worse Off than Dogs." The final spread is a close-up profile of Hamer with a determined look in her eyes. This is a fine introduction to a true American hero. —*Sam Bloom*

2015 WINNER

WOODSON, JACQUELINE. *Brown Girl Dreaming.* Nancy Paulson Books, 2014. Gr. 5–12*

A moving free-verse memoir of Woodson's childhood in Greenville, North Carolina, and Brooklyn recounts family lore and historical events of the turbulent 1960s and 1970s. There are poems about her grandmother's faith (Jehovah's Witness) and her loving grandfather's lack of faith, her baby brother's lead poisoning, an uncle's imprisonment at Rikers Island and his conversion to Islam, as well as poems about friendship and sibling rivalry. Woodson's astute observations through the eyes of her child self are both specific and universal and provide a window to recent American history. Her growing passion for storytelling and writing is evident. In "on paper" (p. 256) she writes: ". . . I know / if I wanted to / I could write anything. / Letters becoming words, words gathering meaning, / becoming / thoughts outside my head."

Lyrical, insightful, touching, powerful, and emotionally charged, Woodson's eloquent poetry is accessible enough to read in one sitting, but young readers and aspiring writers will linger over her vivid vignettes, reliving her memories right along with her. —*Patty Carleton*

2015 HONORS

ALEXANDER, KWAME. *The Crossover.* Houghton Mifflin Harcourt, 2014. Gr. 7–10.

The Crossover is a captivating coming-of-age story written in verse and incorporating visually interesting text. It is perfect for those in the middle grades and beyond and equally suitable for advanced upper-elementary readers.

A contemporary and appealing read covering real-life matters confronting families, it also addresses first love and sibling discord between twelve-year-old twin basketball phenoms, Josh and Jordan. The brothers pick up the game of hoops where their once famous father left off. Alexander skillfully positions basketball as a metaphor for the game of life. Page by engrossing page, the reader is a spectator seated front and center, beholding the play-by-play performances of each character until the final buzzer rings bringing the book to its heartfelt conclusion.

The Crossover scores big on every literary level. Its catchy, quick, and engaging style connects readers of all ages, cultures, and socioeconomic backgrounds, while going into overtime by compelling the most disengaged to get into the game of reading. —*Nichole Shabazz*

NELSON, MARILYN. *How I Discovered Poetry.* Illustrated by Hadley Hooper. Dial, 2014. Gr. 6–10*

Reading Nelson's *How I Discovered Poetry* felt personal . . . like peeking over her shoulder as she records her innermost thoughts. Her powerful command of the language from diary-like musings to those of a uniquely self-aware teen mirrors the development of an extraordinary writer/poet. This slim but powerful memoir spans a critical decade in the life of award-winning poet and literary scholar, Marilyn Nelson. It allows the reader to step back into the 1950s and witness the coming-of-age transformations shared from a keenly observant and impressionable child's point of view.

Each poem, written as a sonnet, strongly establishes a sense of place and time with carefully arranged subtitles emphasizing location and date. The chronological narratives creatively record her family experiences during a period of racial tensions and unrest as they travel via military orders from place to place. The poems reveal a stunning growth from child writer into a thoughtful wordsmith. Some tales are humorous, some clearly poignant—yet they're always deeply self-revealing. Hooper's sketches with strategically placed family photos support Nelson's tightly woven poetry lending authentic design appeal. —*Chrystal Carr Jeter*

MAGOON, KEKLA. *How It Went Down.* Henry Holt, 2014. Gr. 6–12.

Tariq Johnson is a sixteen-year-old African American. A white man shoots and kills him as he leaves a neighborhood convenience store on his way home. The facts surrounding the incident as reported on the news are distorted, but what is the truth? Each character in the story has a different reality. Tariq's death impacts those who witness the killing, those who mourn his death, and those who are affected within and beyond the Underhill neighborhood. Through voices of family, friends, neighbors, and a politician who sees this as an opportunity—and told over the course of nine days—Tariq's story is explored from multiple perspectives. There are no easy answers; there is no justice and little hope of change. Yet a chorus of voices, primarily young people, offers powerful witness to societal breakdowns and to a seemingly intractable cycle of violence. Written as a response to actual news headlines, this book is a catalyst for important dialogue. —*Susan Polos*

2015 JOHN STEPTOE NEW TALENT AWARD

REYNOLDS, JASON. *When I Was the Greatest.* Atheneum, 2014. Gr. 7–12.

Reynolds depicts an inner-city neighborhood in Brooklyn that has its share of drugs, crime, and other problems, but centers on the characters' love, support, and interactions. Main character and narrator, Ali, and friends, nicknamed Noodles and his brother, Needles, who has Tourette syndrome, look out for each other. The brothers survive on their own, without the help of competent parents. The three friends only get into minor issues, until they attend a party that lands them in unexpected trouble. Reynolds relates the boys' story in a strong voice, depicting themes of family, friendship, loyalty, and respect. It is a heart-warming story that reveals themes through characters' dialogue and interactions that never becomes moralistic. —*Christina Dorr*

2014 WINNER

WILLIAMS-GARCIA, RITA. *P.S. Be Eleven*. Amistad/
HarperCollins, 2013. Gr. 4–6.

P.S. Be Eleven picks up where *One Crazy Summer* left off. The reader is immediately immersed
back into the world of the Gaither sisters, Fern,
Vonetta, and Delphine, as they are on their flight
home from meeting their mother. Although *P.S.
Be Eleven* is the second book in the series, this tale
stands alone because Williams-Garcia catches the
reader up on the major events of book one through
the girls' walk through memory lane on their plane trip home. Change is
what awaits the Gaither sisters when they return home: an uncle who has to
readjust to civilian life after returning from the Vietnam War, the engage-
ment of their father, and Delphine has to adjust to a new teacher, all while
going through the trials of being a pre-teen. She writes letters to her mother
to keep her in the loop of all that she experiences. Her mother offers words
that either confuse Delphine or encourage her—yet always reminding her
to be eleven and to not be in a hurry to grow up.

2014 HONORS

LEWIS, JOHN, ANDREW AYDIN, AND NATE POWELL. *March: Book One*.
Top Shelf Productions, 2013. Gr. 4–10*

Freedom. Justice. Equality. What are these words if not examples of what
fighting for civil rights means? In 1963, Martin Luther King Jr. had a dream.
The nation would rise up and hold as self-evident the American truth that
all men are created equal. This dream was shared with Congressman John
Lewis, one of the organizers behind the March on Washington. On the fiftieth anniversary of that dream, staffer Andrew Aydin and comic book writer
Nate Powell embarked on a new project. *March: Book One* tells the story of
the path to social justice and equality. The book opens with an ominous
scene of violence on the Edmund Pettus Bridge in Montgomery, Alabama,
and sets the stage for what would be a journey of social awakening through
comics. March shifts back and forth between the events that led the way

from Congressman Lewis's political awakening to President Obama's inauguration in 2008.

MYERS, WALTER DEAN. *Darius & Twig.* Amistad/HarperCollins, 2013. Gr. 8–12.

Two friends—one African American, one Dominican—navigate their young lives in Harlem amid a jumble of obstacles, including race, violence, family expectations, and personal choice. Darius is the dreamer and writer; Twig, a star runner. Darius and Twig use their talents to defend their ambitions for a better life through their friendship. The slightest misstep could send them down the wrong path and shatter hopes for a future they so strongly hold.

Myers captures realities of life in Harlem in this short novel. He offers a glimpse into the dreams of two contemporary characters—a much-needed perspective in contrast to the stereotypes in media reports today. He documents the bravery of two young men from different backgrounds coming together in a strong friendship made even stronger by their differences and the prejudices that surround them. Myers offers a perspective on negative associations inherent in the sports industry and dangers our youth face in seemingly positive opportunities. As always, he populates this novel with familiar characters: teens who live in the real world, and, who in the case of Darius and Twig, find their way with sensitivity, friendship, and grace.

From *Darius & Twig*

Fury sits on my wrist, and I can feel the power of his talons as he grips the thick leather glove. I am breathing hard but he barely moves, only rocking slightly as he anticipates the hunt. I reach for the string that covers his mask, and taking the other string in my teeth, I loosen it. He turns his head quickly and sees it is me.—*Walter Dean Myers*

GRIMES, NIKKI. *Words with Wings.* Word Song/Boyds Mills, 2013. Gr. 4–10.

Grimes poetically tells the life story of Gabby named after the angel Gabriel by her mother. Gabby is a daydreamer who understands her life through words and poetry. In this universal story of young adolescence Nikki Grimes's word magic makes it possible for the reader to get insight into Gabby's thinking. She shares ordinary things; feeling what she feels when her parents fight, understanding her pain when divorce requires a move, the loss of her only friend, the fright of being the shy newcomer and achieving acceptance of her teacher and eventually her mother. Gabby's writing reflects strong imagery leaving the reader with an appreciation of how words create images. Gabby's lack of attention to events going on around her turns out to be a pathway toward acceptance and understanding by her peers.

2013 WINNER

PINKNEY, ANDREA DAVIS. *Hand in Hand: Ten Black Men Who Changed America.* Illustrated by Brian Pinkney. Jump at the Sun Books, 2012. Gr. 5–8*

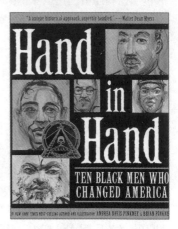

Hand in Hand: Ten Black Men Who Changed America highlights the legacy of ten brave men who saw a need for change in the lives of Black Americans. Each in his own courageous way dared to make a difference. The history is told chronologically from colonial times to the twenty-first century. With the author's unique writing style, each individual is introduced with narration describing how the use of his hands was instrumental in reaching his goal in the fight for justice. A full-page watercolor image of the individual, a contribution from the palette of artist Brian Pinkney, follows the narration. The biographical sketch gives a chronological report of each man's life from childhood until his goal was reached. Those whose stories are included are: Benjamin Banneker, Frederick Douglass, Booker T. Washington, W. E. B. Du Bois, A. Philip Randolph, Thurgood Marshall, Jackie Robinson, Malcolm X, Martin Luther King Jr., and Barack H. Obama II.

> **From *Hand in Hand: Ten Black Men Who Changed America***
>
> These are the stories of ten bold men
> who built a chain called hand in hand.
> Each a link in this mighty strand:
> Reaching
> Pulling

Believing
Achieving
Working toward freedom
Hand in hand.
—*Andrea Davis Pinkney*

2013 HONORS

WOODSON, JACQUELINE. *Each Kindness.* Illustrated by E. B. Lewis. Nancy Paulsen Books, 2012. Gr. K–3.

One winter's day Ms. Albert introduces her class to Maya, a new student who is assigned the desk next to Chloe. After spending the winter ignoring Maya's overtures of friendship, Chloe learns the meaning of kindness and the regrets that come from not being kind.

A wonderful updating of Eleanor Estes's *The Hundred Dresses*, *Each Kindness* is an outstanding example of a "purposeful" book in the hands of a skilled writer. Woodson lets the story unfold without mentally stopping the narrative to point to the lesson. Instead, she trusts that the child reader will understand it. The story is enhanced by E. B. Lewis's illustrations that add to the power of the narrative. Chloe comes to understand her varying emotions from pouty face to regrets in the light of Ms. Albert's lesson on kindness. A strong story for classroom sharing that illuminates the power of each kindness.

From *Each Kindness*

Our teacher Ms. Albert said,
Say good morning to our new student.
But most of us were silent.
The only empty seat was next to me.
That's where our teacher put Maya
And on that first day, Maya turned to me and smiled.
But I didn't smile back.
I moved my chair, myself and my books
a little farther away from her.
When she looked my way, I turned to the window
and stared out at the snow.

And every day after that,
when Maya came into the classroom,
I looked away and didn't smile back.
—*Jacqueline Woodson*

NELSON, VAUNDA MICHEAUX. *No Crystal Stair: A Documentary Novel of the Life and Work of Lewis Michaux, Harlem Bookseller.* Carolrhoda, 2012. Gr. 8–12.

Some of the language in this fictionalized history may shock contemporary readers ("Negro," "colored," and so on), and that's as it should be in this realistic portrait of Black American life in the early to mid-1900s. The story begins in 1906 in Newport News, Virginia, when Lewis was about ten. His wry humor comes through when he learns a lesson about Jesus helping those who make an effort, although not quite the way his mother intended. Readers "mature" along with Lewis as he grows up before coming in to his own as the "Harlem Bookseller," proprietor of the National Memorial African Bookstore, an institution that was much more than a store. This groundbreaking enterprise focused on Black literature, readers, and writers, and offered a community hub for people interested in current affairs, particularly civil rights.

Varying points of view keep the first-person narrative interesting, some voices are those of real historical figures, including Lewis himself, his brothers, Nikki Giovanni, and others; some are fictional. An index helps identify what is factual. Archival images—again, some factual, some not—of newspaper articles, advertisements, FBI reports, photos of the store and prominent people who visited it are interspersed throughout these narratives and add flavor to the period, as do black-and-white spot sketches.

This account doesn't sugarcoat what life was like for its subject, Lewis Michaux, and many other Americans at that time; yet, it is an inspiring and uplifting history lesson, even better for being couched in such a gripping read.

From *No Crystal Stair*

I am interested in going into the book business and approach Carter G. Woodson for guidance. His stellar reputation in scholarly circles and connection with the *Negro History Journal* led me to his doorstep. "I'm a historian. I'm a writer. I am not a seller of books," Mr. Woodson said when I met him. "The man you need to interview about Negro book sales is Michaux in New York."

Woodson was right. Lewis Michaux knows about books . . . and selling. And he shared his knowledge with enthusiasm. A trifle self-impressed but a fascinating man, and his National Memorial African Bookstore is a literary treasure. —*Vaunda Micheaux Nelson*

2012 WINNER

NELSON, KADIR. *Heart and Soul: The Story of America and African Americans.* Harper-Collins, 2011. Gr. 3–7*

Kadir Nelson's *Heart and Soul* is true to its title. In words and illustrations, it tells the story of Americans and African Americans brought to this foreign soil against their will. The text balances the ugliness of slavery against the contributions of African Americans in the building of this great nation, proving their endurance and perseverance while striving to become first-class citizens. Included in the story are references to Martin Luther King Jr.'s "I Have a Dream" speech at the 1963 March on Washington, the 1964 signing of the Civil Rights Act, and the 1965 Voting Rights Act. The vibrant colors in the paintings that open each chapter depict some of the actual freedom-based events in the history of this country. The final illustration—a pair of wrinkled hands holding a patriotically designed pin saying, "I voted"—may be the hands of the narrator who had the opportunity to vote for the first African American President of the United States, Barack Obama.

From *Heart and Soul*

Life on the frontier was rough. In most parts there weren't any trees, so folks had to build their homes out of mud bricks and cow pies. For fresh water they had to dig wells. They grew their vegetables and hunted for food. Every day on those flat prairies was a fight to survive, but fighting to live as a free person out there was always better than living under the whip on a southern plantation. —*Kadir Nelson*

2012 HONORS

GREENFIELD, ELOISE. *The Great Migration: Journey to the North.* Illustrated by Jan Spivey Gilchrist. Amistad/HarperCollins, 2011. Gr. 3–5.

Collage illustrations pair beautifully with these evocative poems. Maps, old photos, and woodblock prints blend images. The poem entitled "The Trip" shows a picture of a steam train going past a cornfield. Images of people are camouflaged by the cornstalks. Emotions of the travelers clearly reflect what they are feeling. In "Goodbyes Man," the man is shown with his head down, arms folded. The accompanying poem tells us "Saying goodbye to the land / puts a pain on my heart."

It's tempting for those of us on this side of history to assume everyone was happy to escape the unjust social order so prominent in the American South in the early 1900s. In truth, people who did so took great risks in leaving everything they knew behind for an unsure future. "Question" poses aptly each traveler's worry: "Will I make a good life / for my family, / for myself?"

Young readers would benefit from some contextual knowledge before dipping into these narratives. An author's note at the beginning provides some historical information. Greenfield's poems and Gilchrist's art effectively personalize this significant historical era.

From *The Great Migration: Journey to the North*

They hear the whistle blow.
It blows again, not so far away.
They see the train coming closer
and closer, and then it stops. They gather
on the platform, hold out their tickets,
climb aboard. "All aboard!"
the conductor calls. It's time.
They're moving slowly,
then faster, some think too fast,
some think not fast enough,
toward a world they don't yet know.
—*Eloise Greenfield*

MCKISSACK, PATRICIA C. *Never Forgotten.* Illustrated by Leo and Diane Dillon. Schwartz and Wade, 2011. Gr. 4–8.

Master storyteller Patricia McKissack creates a provocative, heartwrenching saga that portrays the anguish of slavery, especially that of the parents who had their children taken from them. Told in verse, this cycle of poems combines history, folklore, and mysticism to deliver a message of hope and of the importance of family.

In West Africa in 1725, Musafa is born to Dinga, a talented and respected seventh-generation blacksmith. When Musafa's mother dies in childbirth, his father uses his gift of magic to personify the four elements of nature—fire, earth, wind, and water—to assist in his son's upbringing. By a twist of fate, when Musafa is enjoying the pleasures of freedom, he is captured by foreigners and ends up as a slave in South Carolina. With the help of the Mother Elements, who travel across the ocean to uncover his whereabouts, Dinga is informed that his son is alive and using the skills he was taught as a young boy. He finds comfort in this knowledge. Dramatic, stylized acrylic and watercolor illustrations perfectly frame the story and add to the sense of magical realism.

From *Never Forgotten*

Musafa,
Sold.
See him no more.
Hear him no more.
Shum Da Da We Da Shum Da Da We Da.
—*Patricia C. McKissack*

2011 WINNER

WILLIAMS-GARCIA, RITA. *One Crazy Summer.* Amistad/HarperCollins, 2010. Gr. 3–7.

Historical fiction at its best, *One Crazy Summer* brings the summer of 1968 into brilliant focus through the lives of Delphine and her two sisters, Vonetta and Fern. They learn to live for the summer in a new place with a mother they barely

know. Flying to Oakland, California, where the girls have to avoid making a spectacle of themselves while they keep count of the Black people on the plane and in the airport, is just the first part of their summer of growth. The girls react to their new life with confidence and skepticism: who are these men in berets who visit their mother, Cecile? Why does everyone else call her Sister Nzila? What is this Black Panther day camp? Why does their mother expect them to fend for themselves? How can they stay true to their father's and grandmother's instruction and still find their own way? Characters are fully and honestly developed, making these three sisters some of the most memorable in children's literature. Delphine tells the story, full of love and humor and strength, and the young reader is left to revel in the world of 1968. Pair with *The Rock and the River* by Kekla Magoon (CSK Steptoe Winner, 2010) for a first introduction to the complexities of the Black Panther Party.

From *One Crazy Summer*

Sister Mukumbu announced, "Today we're going to be like the earth, spinning around and affecting many. Today we're going to think about our part in the revolution." Vonetta's hand shot up. I kicked her under the table, but she was determined to have everyone look at her, which meant having everyone look at us. I forgot all about Hirohito and was afraid of what Vonetta would say next: and sure enough, Vonetta said, "We didn't come for the revolution. We came for breakfast." Then Fern added "And to meet our mother in Oakland." —*Rita Williams-Garcia*

2011 HONORS

MYERS, WALTER DEAN. *Lockdown.* Harper Teen/Amistad, 2010. Gr. 7–10.

Reese's story takes place in a juvenile detention facility, and in typical Myers fashion, the context is not sugarcoated or romanticized. While completing work release in a nursing home, Reese forges a relationship with an elderly man who offers insight into Reese's struggle despite very different life experiences. This intergenerational relationship pushes Reese to question racism, both in the present and the past, and reflect on his own choices.

Throughout Reese's story, big questions and moral dilemmas are debated. Should Reese help a younger detainee who is being bullied? Is there any way to hold the guards accountable for their corruption? How can Reese simultaneously stay connected to his community and family (particularly his little sister) while staying safe and out of trouble? Myers does not provide easy answers. For readers who will experience this book as a window, Reese's story offers insight and honesty. For readers who will experience the story as a mirror, Reese's story offers authenticity and compassion. This novel is graphic in its portrayal of violence and use of language.

From *Lockdown*

She was kidding around with me and I liked it. At Progress nobody kidded around with you. Even when you were talking to your friends it could change in a minute. You said the wrong thing and somebody would get mad and swing at you, or they were having a bad day and you didn't know it, or their medication wasn't working. You could never tell. —*Walter Dean Myers*

RHODES, JEWELL PARKER. *Ninth Ward.* Little, Brown, 2010. Gr. 5–8.

Mystical story elements and a realistic narrative paint a compelling picture of Hurricane Katrina's aftermath. Twelve-year-old Lanesha is left to survive the storm with her "Mama Ya-Ya" in their Ninth Ward neighborhood. Everyone knows a storm is coming. Only Mama Ya-Ya with the "sight" knows that the storm itself isn't the biggest threat. The subsequent failure of the levees is what doomed the Ninth Ward. Mama Ya-Ya's eerie premonitions effectively evoke the apprehension she feels.

Lanesha's bond with Mama Ya-Ya, who has taken her in after her mother dies in childbirth and her biological family rejects her, is strong. Lanesha's wealthier family does not remember her birthday nor comes to help when the population is told to evacuate. Horrifying details aren't spared. One friend goes to the Superdome and is separated from his family; others leave the city; still others are never heard from again, and just as happened in real life, it's unknown whether they lived or died.

From *Ninth Ward*

The TV flashes pictures "The highways are bumper-to-bumper," says a male reporter. "When gas runs out, they just get out and walk. See, that family there. Hitchhiking. Thousands of folks are trying to leave New Orleans." Another picture. "Even though it's a mandatory evacuation, the mayor is allowing those who don't have the money to leave to spend the night in the Superdome." I lean forward, trying to see if I can see TaShon or Ginia in the sea of people on the screen. —*Jewell Parker Rhodes*

NERI, GREG. *Yummy: The Last Days of a Southside Shorty.* Illustrated by Randy DuBurke. Lee and Low, 2010. Gr. 8–12*

Who was "Yummy" and why at eleven years of age did he end up a gang leader responsible for the death of fourteen-year-old Shavon Dean? Was he a victim of his circumstances or a cold-blooded killer who got what he deserved? Based on facts, Robert "Yummy" Sandifer, a boy who loved sweets, grew up on Chicago's South Side, where being a gang member was the only way to survive. Told through the eyes of a fictional observer, Yummy accidently kills his neighbor and for three days becomes a fugitive from the law with very little hope for survival. This powerful and stirring graphic novel will haunt the reader as it grapples with difficult questions of right and wrong that have no easy answers. Bold, evocative black-and-white drawings complement this gritty, award-winning saga that needs to be told.

From *Yummy: The Last Days of a Southside Shorty*

You ready to take the black disciples nation pledge? I guess so . . . better guess again. I wanna be a black disciple! All right then, little man, let's do it. Hold up your right hand. Your other right hand. —*Greg Neri*

2011 JOHN STEPTOE NEW TALENT AWARD

BOND, VICTORIA, AND T. R. SIMON. *Zora and Me.* Candlewick Press, 2010. Gr. 5–8.

This book is a fictionalized account of the childhood of Zora Neale Hurston, the renowned Harlem Renaissance writer. Carrie Brown, Zora's best friend, narrates events of the summer prior to fourth grade. The girls have a fantastical adventure with king alligators, a strange murder, and family mysteries. The events take place in Florida during the early 1900s in the small town of Eatonville, a close-knit rural community of African Americans.

The two girls witness the fate of a young man who was foolish enough to try to wrestle Ghost, king of the gators. The incident piqued Zora's imagination so when she sees Mr. Pendir appear to have a gator head and a man's body, Zora and her friends investigate the frightening events that seem related to this magical shape-changing man. When an elderly woman falls near the swimming hole and a man is murdered near their town, they are sure Mr. Pendir is involved.

The story reads like a folktale of strange creatures and brave children who challenge them. The character, Gold, who passes for white, is rare in children's books. One of the strengths of this novel is the support of adults who interact with the children. The book includes a biography and timeline of Zora Neale Hurston's life.

From *Zora and Me*

I saw it. That night at the Blue Sink, I saw Mr. Pendir with a gator snout plain as I see you right now. It can't be no accident that Old Lady Bronson—a woman who's never been sick a day in her life—fainted and fell, and Mr. Pendir only a few hundred yards away! —*Victoria Bond and T. R. Simon*

2010 WINNER

NELSON, VAUNDA MICHEAUX. *Bad News for Outlaws: The Remarkable Life of Bass Reeves, Deputy U.S. Marshal.* Illustrated by R. Gregory Christie. Carolrhoda, 2009. Gr. 3–5*

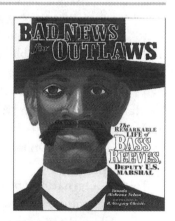

Stunning oil paintings and fluid storytelling come together in a rip-roaring tale of heroism, bravery, and adventure in the late 1800s. Born into slavery in Texas, Bass Reeves fled his owner during the Civil War and lived with Indians, learning all he needed to know to become a deputy U.S. marshal. This well-researched biography reads like great fiction, complete with the tone and rhythm of a tall tale. Bass was a straight-shooting, honest marshal for thirty-two years, arresting more than 3,000 outlaws with only fourteen deaths. Christie's paintings capture the personality of the no-nonsense, clever, and respectable Bass. His eyes shift while he plans his captures, surprises the bad guys, and arrests his own son. One special illustration shows Bass aiming his gun at the outlaw Jim Webb, who has just put a bullet through the marshal's cowboy hat. Never flinching from the realities of slavery, lynching, and racism, Nelson and Christie tell the story of a strong black man who defied the odds and became a legend. Modern children need to know his story and this fine biography is the perfect place to start. Generous endnotes include a bibliography and fascinating author's note.

From *Bad News for Outlaws*

Jim Webb's luck was running muddy when Bass Reeves rode into town. Webb had stayed one jump ahead of the lawman for two years. He wasn't about to be caught now. Packing both rifle and revolver, the desperado leaped out a window of Bywaters' store. He made a break for his horse, but Reeves cut him off. —*Vaunda Micheaux Nelson*

2010 HONOR

DAVIS, TANITA S. *Mare's War*. Knopf, 2009. Gr. 6–10.

Road trip! One summer, sisters Octavia and Tali are forced to ride across country with their unconventional grandmother to the family reunion. It is not a trip to be enjoyed but endured. Octavia and Tali like to complain and are often disagreeable. When Mare opens up to them about her life, the trip becomes an adventure. Octavia and Tali didn't know their grandmother had run away from home and joined the Army as a teenager. Mesmerized by Mare's experiences in World War II, the sisters become less self-absorbed and argumentative. Previously untold stories of African American military women, and their own family history, transform the road trip into a meaningful life experience.

Told in alternating voices and times—then and now—Davis's smooth transition from the past to the present keeps pace with the changing scenery. Octavia and Tali's teenage attitude, behavior, and voice are very real and their responses evolve as they become more sensitive to the world outside of their own friends and interests.

From *Mare's War*

What happens if I forget how to use my mask? If I get that gas in my lungs, it will kill me dead. I hear about folk who didn't duck fast enough when those grenades came in and got their hands and arms and legs blown clean off. I can't go to France. I can't go where they're throwing them grenades. I can't go and leave Fern. I can't. I can't. —*Tanita S. Davis*

2010 JOHN STEPTOE NEW TALENT AWARD

MAGOON, KEKLA. *The Rock and the River.* Aladdin/Simon & Schuster, 2009. Gr. 6–8.

Demonstrations, marches, and other nonviolent tactics have almost taken over the life of thirteen-year-old Samuel Childs, son of a well-known African American civil rights leader in Chicago. Sam struggles with his father's strict discipline, a sheltered home life, and society's racial injustices. He loves and admires his seventeen-year-old Black Panther brother Steven (known as Stick) who is rebelling against their parents' middle class lifestyle.

Bucky, one of Stick's friends is beaten and falsely arrested by the police. The community erupts in militant protest. Sam has witnessed the police brutality and discovered a handgun hidden in the bedroom they shared. Sam feels helpless and unable to do anything about this miscarriage of justice. On the day of Bucky's trial, Sam's father organizes a peaceful demonstration, with Stick and the Black Panthers present. Sam is torn between non-violence and hard-hitting action. Will he be a stable rock or follow the river's path of motion and change?

This coming-of-age story recreates the tensions of the 1960's Civil Rights Movement and the emotions of young activists. While the Black Panther's militant stance is well known by many, their social programs like free breakfast and health care are often overlooked. An historical overview of the Civil Rights Movement and the Black Panther Party can be found at the end of the book.

From *The Rock and the River*

"Explain what happened tonight," she said. "Pick up your head and look at me." "Yes, mama." I breathed deeply and looked in her eyes. I couldn't lie to her. She knew. Somehow, she already knew. "I went to a political education class."

"What were you thinking?" Father's granite demand placed the last straw on the load I was carrying.

I spun toward him. "What do you want from me?" I shouted.

Father's stunned expression sucked the fight out of me. I'd never talked back to him. Never. He gazed at me with slacked incredulity. I had shocked him into silence, and that was saying something. —*Kekla Magoon*

2009 WINNER

NELSON, KADIR. *We Are the Ship: The Story of Negro League Baseball.* Jump at the Sun/Hyperion Books for Children, 2008. Gr. 3–8*

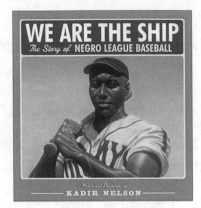

"Seems like we've been playing baseball for a mighty long time. At least as long as we've been free" begins the story of a remarkable group of men dedicated to a sport that did everything in its power to exclude them. Kadir Nelson tells the mesmerizing story of the African American community's passion for and dedication to baseball. Divided into nine innings, each records a different aspect of the history of Negro League Baseball.

The story begins in the mid-1860s and travels forward to 1920, when Andrew "Rube" Foster, "an old-time trick pitcher," arrives on the scene to organize what became the Negro National League. Well-known players like Josh Gibson and Satchel Paige, as well as lesser-known players like George "Mule" Suttles and Norman "Turkey" Stearns, come to life. Inning by inning, Nelson recalls the hardships of traveling through a racist South and the thrill of the crowd when the fast-moving "bunt-and-run" play, an invention credited to Foster, proved successful. A bibliography, endnotes, and index verify the work's authenticity, but it is Nelson's talent as a wordsmith that brings this story to life for baseball lovers and history buffs of all ages.

From *We Are the Ship*

People ask all the time if we are bitter because we weren't given the chance to play baseball in the major leagues for all of those years. Some of us are, but most of us aren't. Most Negroes back then had to work in factories, wash windows, or work some man's plantation, and they didn't get paid much for it. We were fortunate men. We got to play baseball for a living, something we would have done if we hadn't gotten paid for it. When you can do what you love to do and get paid for it, it's a wonderful thing.
—*Kadir Nelson*

2009 HONORS

SMITH, HOPE ANITA. *Keeping the Night Watch.* Illustrated by E. B. Lewis. Henry Holt, 2008. Gr. 6–8.

This narrative poem continues the saga begun in *The Way a Door Closes* (2003), as family members deal with Father, who returns home as abruptly as he left. Daughter Zuri views his return with both joy and fear, feelings that manifest themselves when she names her pillow dog "Stay." Bryon joins his father in a pickup game of hoops as if he'd never been gone; Momma goes about the house "wearing a painted smile on her face"; and C.J. is filled with anger, having lost his position as man of the house: "I'm a pot with the lid on / I keep all my mad inside." Yet, with the changing seasons, the household changes. C.J., in a fragile truce with his father, experiences the pangs of young love; readers are introduced to the quieting presence of Maya: "Preacher claims I'm a thief because I steal glances at her and store them in my head." Smith's moving prose poem about a family in turmoil does not lull readers with an all's-well ending, but there's a faint light at the end—a message of hope for young people who may be in a similar situation.

> **From *Keeping the Night Watch***
>
> I take my Daddy's hand and I start to dance
> with him
> around the room.
> We laugh
> hard
> and the water that flows from our eyes
> flows into one big river,
> but we are not afraid . . .
> We keep our eyes on Him.
> We dance on our tears
> —From "Dance with Me," Hope Anita Smith

THOMAS, JOYCE CAROL. *The Blacker the Berry: Poems.* Illustrated by Floyd Cooper. HarperCollins, 2008. Gr. K–3.

Black as a single color has been lauded in prose and poetry across time: "Black is the color of my true love's hair"; "Yet do I marvel at this thing, / To make a poet black and bid him sing." Joyce Carol Thomas expands black into a kaleidoscope of colors in poems that speak to children of every shade. A message of rejoicing comes from a "biscuit brown" child, and a salute to "raspberry black" recognizes Native Americans, here "from the first seed." Floyd Cooper's energetic illustrations capture the exuberance of the young people who rejoice in their color birthright. Thomas is highly deserving of the Coretta Scott King honor for her tribute to the beauty of "all the colors of the race," a positive message that speaks to readers everywhere.

> **From *The Blacker the Berry***
>
> We are color struck
> The way an artist strikes
> His canvas with his brush of many hues
> Look closely at these mirrors
> these palettes of skin
> Each color is rich
> in its own right . . .
> We come in all shades
> —*From "Color Struck," Joyce Carol Thomas*

WEATHERFORD, CAROLE BOSTON. *Becoming Billie Holiday.* Illustrated by Floyd Cooper. Wordsong/Boyds Mills Press, 2008. Gr. 6–9*

Born in Philadelphia in 1915 to a teenage mother, Billie Holiday experienced poverty, discrimination, heartbreak, and parental neglect. By the time she was twenty-five, she was a legend in the world of music. Billie quit school in the fifth grade. She worked at a wide range of jobs from being a maid to prostitution. As a teenager, she realized she had a good singing voice and made her way to Harlem. By the age of sixteen, she was singing with famous bandleaders such as Teddy Wilson, Artie Shaw, and Duke Ellington. Weatherford tells the singer's story in a fictionalized verse memoir using the titles of Holiday's songs to head her ninety-seven poems.

Holiday's troubles in school, feelings about music, her mother, her absent father, and the various places where she lived reflect her longing for love and attention. Other famous people who were important in her life included Count Basie, Duke Ellington, and Paul Robeson. Holiday's own voice, written as if spoken from childhood to about age twenty-five, provides a personal sense of the singer. The final poem, titled "Coda: Strange Fruit," is an acknowledgment of Holiday's signature song, "Strange Fruit."

From *Becoming Billie Holiday*

No one taught me to sing just behind the beat,
to tease listeners with my tempo,
to glide above the band, flit between
musicians like a canary finally free.
No one trained me to blow like a horn,
to milk a measure by bending the melody,
to breathe a universe in a single note,
and end a song in a different key . . .
That came natural, baby. That all came natural.
—From *"I Gotta Right to Sing the Blues,"* Carole Boston Weatherford

2008 WINNER

CURTIS, CHRISTOPHER PAUL. *Elijah of Buxton.* Scholastic, 2007. Gr. 3–6.

The town of Buxton, located a few miles from the Detroit River in Canada, was a community founded as a destination for slaves who traveled the Underground Railroad to freedom. Twelve-year-old Elijah was the first child born free in Buxton. His tender heart and spirit led him to be described as "fra-gile." Despite this failing, Elijah had two unique skills: fishing without hook or line and deciphering language. When Elijah and his friend Cooter see their teacher's planned topic on the blackboard: "familiarity breeds contempt," they are all in. Using all the context clues they can muster, they decide that the teacher will be speaking about a "family breeding contest," and they don't want to miss a minute.

The scars of slavery exist side by side with opportunity to live free. Work ethics, sense of community, and unrelenting effort to raise funds to buy freedom for those left in bondage are ever present. When Preacher Zephariah convinces Mr. Leroy that he can successfully barter the freedom of Leroy's wife and children, a midnight whirlwind of lies, grim examples of servitude, and dangerous situations ensue. "Fra-gile" Elijah is right in the middle. Elijah of Buxton is a coming-of-age historical read about a time and place where few writers have ventured.

From *Elijah of Buxton*

Whenever new-free folk come to live in Buxton, we ring the bell twenty times for each one of 'em. Ten times to ring out their old lives and ten more to ring in their new ones, their free lives. Then, we ask the new-free folks to, one by one, climb the ladder of the steeple and rub the bell with their left hand. Most times when you're doing something important you're supposed to use your right hand, but we ask 'em to use their left hand 'cause it's closest to their hearts. —*Christopher Paul Curtis*

2008 HONORS

DRAPER, SHARON M. *November Blues.* Atheneum, 2007. Gr. 9–12.

There were three things of which November was sure: Josh was dead; Josh was her "baby daddy"; and she, November, was pregnant. What was unsure was how to tell her mother, what to do with a baby, and rethinking her plans for college on scholarship. Draper tells a poignant story of one thoughtless moment and its effect not only on the protagonist but also on all who are in this circle. November's mother moves between anger, disappointment, and motherly concern. Josh's parents have designs on adopting the baby, decrying November as an unfit mother. Jericho, Josh's cousin, a talented musician and best friend, pledges to be November's ardent supporter. In his grief, he puts down his trumpet and joins the football team, convincing himself that he need only "sweat and run tackle!"

Draper shares the complexities of having a baby—the physical concerns before, during, and after, endless financial responsibilities, the physical care, and the effects on all concerned. Draper offers no easy answers. Despite November's problems, the book includes moments of high drama, humor, and laughable boy-girl scenarios.

From *November Blues*

"That's some nice music you're playing," Olivia said as she relaxed into the sofa cushions. "I like the blues." She closed her eyes.

November nodded, "I used to think it was dumb, old-timey music. Maybe you gotta deal with some stuff before you can really feel the blues." She looked at Olivia, and the two girls exchanged knowing glances. —*Sharon M. Draper*

SMITH, CHARLES R., JR. *Twelve Rounds to Glory: The Story of Muhammad Ali.* Illustrated by Bryan Collier. Candlewick Press, 2007. Gr. 5–9*

In twelve chapters, illustrated by Bryan Collier, Smith's epic-style poem, influenced by the rhythms of rap, describes Muhammad Ali's life, values, and public persona. Smith's poetry reflects admiration for his subject— not only for his prowess in boxing, but also for his personal expressions of Black pride. Ali's fight against discrimination and segregation was not just the pugilist speaking, but also a man standing fast with his pacifist credo. As he faces the loss of his world championship title and banishment from the ring, Ali says no to war, reinforcing his dedication to the tenets of his Islamic religion. Smith captures Ali's voice teasing and taunting his opponents, using his well-known penchant for poetry to express himself.

Phrases in large black print decorate the pages, emphasizing chapter titles and Ali's words: "'Eat your words! Eat your words! I am the king! I'm the king of the world!'" Later chapters cover Ali's personal life, four marriages, eight children, the diagnosis of Parkinson's disease, and that unforgettable moment when he carries the torch to light the cauldron at the 1996 Atlanta Olympic Games. An informative time line of Ali's life through 2005 completes this graphic, poetic presentation.

From *Twelve Rounds to Glory*

Round TWELVE—Muhammad on the Mountain
Holding the Olympic torch
with a warrior spirit,
you reignited memories
of the champ who never quit
in the ring,
in life,

using substance and style,
now a gentle gladiator
with a sparkling smile,
you lit the Olympic cauldron
glowing golden in the night
and became a supernova
bathed in beautiful light.
—*Charles R. Smith Jr.*

2008 JOHN STEPTOE NEW TALENT AWARD

FRAZIER, SUNDEE T. *Brendan Buckley's Universe and Everything in It.* Delacorte, 2007. Gr. 3–5.

Meet Brendan Buckley, lively ten-year-old, maybe a budding scientist, striving to please the master in his tae kwon do class, sharing mischief with his buddy, Khalfani, and missing his late grandfather, Clem. Life seems just about okay until Brendan stops at a rock exhibit in the mall. He is talking to the exhibitor when with sudden swiftness his grandmother Gladys pulls him abruptly away, just as the "rock" man was about to sell him a calcite. Yet another strange thing—the name on the man's card was the same as his mother's maiden name: DuBose. Could there be a connection between Gladys's actions, the name of the gentleman who happened to be white, and his mother's reaction when Brendan arrives home? Undaunted by the silence at home, Brendan and Khalfani do some detective work, find a way to Mr. DuBose's home, and finally get to the bottom of the behavior on everyone's part. The end of the story is skillfully crafted. There is no sudden "happily ever after" in the family relationships, but the reader is left knowing that things will turn out all right in this cross-generational, multicultural tale.

From *Brendan Buckley's Universe and Everything in It*

I flipped back a couple of pages and found the reason I'd opened the book in the first place. I checked off the question "What am I?"

Here is What I Found Out: I am a scientist, a mineral collector, a sometimes Noble Tae Kwon Do warrior, a friend, a son, a grandson, someone who belongs to both black and white people, a mixture like a rock, my color, but—much more—myself. —*Sundee T. Frazier*

2007 WINNER

DRAPER, SHARON M. *Copper Sun.* Atheneum, 2006. Gr. 9–12.

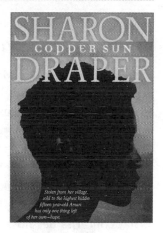

Day broke like any other day in Amari's African village, but before the sun went down her life had tragically changed. Slavers looted the village, killed or captured the villagers, and led the captives on a tormented journey in the dark hold of a slave ship. Fifteen-year-old Amari is eventually sold to a plantation owner as a birthday present for his sixteen-year-old son Clay. As Amari's story unfolds, the life-threatening activities on the plantation, her degradation as Clay's sex object, the cold-blooded murder of an innocent newborn, and the disquieting relationship between Amari and Polly, an indentured servant, are revealed. The opportunity to escape encourages Amari, Polly, and the child, Tidbit, to seek the safe haven of Fort Mose in St. Augustine, Florida.

Classified as fiction, this page-turner is based on impeccable research of the lives of those who were captured as slaves in eighteenth-century America. Throughout the burdensome, physically and emotionally painful life she led as a slave, Amari never lost her dream of once again being free.

From *Copper Sun*

A large woman came and sat down next to her and offered her a small piece of her own portion. Amari took it gratefully.

"Crying won't help, child," she told her. "This place is slimy with tears."

Amari was surprised to hear the woman speak in her own Ewe language. She wiped her eyes and said in barely a whisper, "I feel like a broken drum—hollow, crushed, unable to make a sound."

"You must learn to make music once more."

. . .

"So why should I endure this? Why did you not let me just die in there?" Amari cried out.

"Because I see a power in you." Afi lifted her shackled wrist and reached over to touch Amari. "You know, certain people are chosen to survive. I don't know why, but you are one of those who must remember the past and tell those yet unborn. You must live." —*Sharon M. Draper*

2007 HONOR

GRIMES, NIKKI. *The Road to Paris.* G. P. Putnam's Sons, 2006. Gr. 4–8.

Paris and her brother Malcolm endured a tough childhood and now live with their grandmother in a small apartment. Their grandmother cannot provide the peace and safety they seek. The siblings are separated, Malcolm to an unknown destination and Paris to a foster family in upstate New York. The Lincolns, with two boys of their own and another foster daughter, aren't perfect, but they show Paris the patience and generosity she so desperately needs. Inbred community racism doesn't dominate Paris's life. She has already felt its sting as a biracial child abandoned by her white father. What concerns her now is whether to give her alcoholic mother a second chance. Singing in the church choir, the support of other children, and finding a belief in God help Paris develop trust and eventually discover a home inside herself.

Faith is a real part of Paris's growing ability to handle life confidently, yet Grimes's quiet portrayal doesn't leave out the prejudice or hurt. The tender poignancy of Paris's internal voice powerfully reveals the strength of a child discovering herself, flourishing, and learning to use her gifts.

From *The Road to Paris*

Paris sat swinging her legs, pouting—until she heard the first chords of the organ. The sound sent an electric spark up one pew and down the next, and Paris forgot all about being cold. The melody flowed into her body like liquid sunshine, warming her as it traveled from the tips of her ears to the tips of her toes. Paris never knew that such a sound existed.

"Are you okay?" asked Mr. Lincoln. Paris, her lips slightly parted, nodded and went on listening. She didn't know how to explain it, but as the music played, she felt herself waking up inside. —*Nikki Grimes*

2007 JOHN STEPTOE NEW TALENT AWARD

JONES, TRACI L. *Standing Against the Wind.* Farrar, Straus and Giroux, 2006. Gr. 6–9.

In this first novel, protagonist Patrice, a thirteen-year-old, is suddenly moved from the security of her grandmother's home in rural Georgia to the bustling city of Chicago. Her mother is sent to jail, and Patrice finds shelter in a small apartment with her mother's sister and three young cousins. She is now responsible for doing chores around the home, holding afternoon school for her cousins, and struggling to maintain her grades. Patrice must also deal with the constant harassment of neighborhood gangs and youthful drug dealers. Monty, living in the same building, comes to her rescue, beginning an abiding friendship.

Patrice learns that her grades make her eligible for a prestigious scholarship. There is only one hitch. Her mother, in jail many miles away, must sign the application. With Monty at her side, a determined Patrice stands up against many seemingly insurmountable obstacles. Monty admires Patrice's academic abilities and is encouraged to improve his own study habits. His personal ingenuity is instrumental in securing Patrice's scholarship. Tense moments, tender moments, and moments of adult encouragement combine to make *Standing Against the Wind* a real page-turner.

From *Standing Against the Wind*

"Your watch. It was such a nice watch. I can't believe you sold it."

But to Patrice it was a really big deal. He had taken the one thing of value that he owned and sold it for her. . . .

Patrice looked at him. And for the third time that day, she kissed him.
—*Traci L. Jones*

2006 WINNER

LESTER, JULIUS. *Day of Tears: A Novel in Dialogue.* Jump at the Sun/Hyperion Books for Children, 2005. Gr. 9–12.

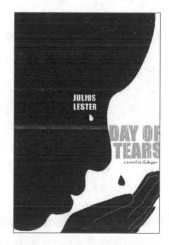

Lester's fictionalized account of the largest slave auction in U.S. history, held in 1859 in Savannah, Georgia, makes immediate and personal the horror of the event. In a powerfully dramatic format, the voices of enslaved Africans and their masters move between monologues and conversations. Lester's sparing words always seem vividly to illuminate each character. Begging to be staged, this work makes clear the moral dilemmas inherent in the slave auction. The inhumanity of the process is strengthened by characters who speak years down the line, giving a broad perspective and bringing a kind of closure to the happenings. The challenge to affirm our humanity in this most inhumane situation is reflected in the somber words and setting: the rain comes down like fiery sorrow, rain like needles on your skin or rain as hard as regret. As the character Mattie says, "This ain't rain. This is God's tears."

From *Day of Tears*

Mattie: I look at the slave-seller sitting beside Master Butler. There's a toothpick sticking out of the left corner of his mouth. He takes a sip of coffee without moving that toothpick out of the way. He eats with that toothpick bobbing up and down. I wish he'd stop looking at Emma like she's a hog and he's trying to figure how many pork chops and slabs of bacon he can get out of her. —*Julius Lester*

2006 HONORS

BOLDEN, TONYA. *Maritcha: A Nineteenth-Century American Girl.* Harry N. Abrams, 2005. Gr. 4–7*

Maritcha Lyons was born to free Black parents who owned their own boardinghouse in New York City. Her family enjoyed leisurely, fun-filled outings and the company of many famous friends and guests, including Frederick Douglass. Maritcha's parents acquired a piano for her and paid for lessons to keep her spirits up while she recovered from illness. However, with all this seeming affluence, Maritcha was well aware of the difficulties faced by Blacks. "'At anti-slavery meetings and conferences, mother was almost invariably present,' Maritcha remembered, 'not to agitate but to learn her duty.'" This duty was being an ace operator for the Underground Railroad. But the lifestyle Maritcha and her family enjoyed could not keep them from their own difficulties. They lost everything in the New York City draft riots of 1863. A mob torched their home and the family was forced to flee. Eventually they relocated in Providence, Rhode Island, where Maritcha became the first Black person to graduate from the all-white Providence High School.

Author Bolden, using enhancing reproductions from Maritcha Lyons's unpublished memoir, has crafted a handsome biography, replete with contemporaneous illustrations. It is a well-documented narrative with source notes, bibliography, and illustration and text credits.

From *Maritcha*

She took part in school activities, such as playing the piano for the choral club. But Maritcha kept her guard up. "The iron had entered my soul. I never forgot that I had to sue for a privilege which any but a colored girl could have without asking." —*Tonya Bolden*

GRIMES, NIKKI. *Dark Sons.* Jump at the Sun/Hyperion Books for Children, 2005. Gr. 5–8.

Grimes's novel in verse is a portrait of two young men who both feel betrayed by their fathers. Each father—one in ancient biblical times, one in a contemporary setting—has moved on to start a new family with "another woman." The biblical Ishmael and Sam, born in Brooklyn, New York, wonder if God has forsaken them and the mother who cares for them. Grimes's poetic word pictures of two damaged young men, told in alternating voices, are both heartbreaking and healing. As the stories parallel each other (a slight change in print marking the separation), a reader might ask: Are there no new stories under the sun? Introducing a story from a religious tradition to contemporary audiences of multicultural traditions, Grimes skillfully makes the leap from the past to the present in a way that is entirely credible.

From *Dark Sons*

When I am angriest,
His is the hand
that calms me,
the one that rests
on my shoulder invisibly,
pressing patience
into my very bones,
letting me know
it is all right
to breathe.
—*from "Silent Solace" Nikki Grimes*

Moody as midnight,
I pound minor keys
on electric piano.
I am here to lose myself
in the music,
to jam with Jesus—
the only one
who hasn't let me down
so far.
—*from "Band Practice," Nikki Grimes*

NELSON, MARILYN. *A Wreath for Emmett Till.* Illustrated by Philippe Lardy. Houghton Mifflin, 2005. Gr. 9–12*

Emmett Louis Till was a lively fourteen-year-old African American boy who was lynched in August 1955 near Money, Mississippi, for allegedly whistling at a white woman. His mother, Mamie Till, held an open-casket funeral for all to witness the horror of her son's death. A photograph of his mangled body, published in *Jet* magazine, became a catalyst for the Civil Rights Movement of the late 1950s and 1960s.

A Wreath for Emmett Till is Nelson's poetic response to "innocence slaughtered by the hands of hate," mourning Till's loss and hinting at the life he might have had. Back matter explains the author's allusions and the symbolism of the flowers in the wreath. A Wreath for Emmett Till is structured as a "heroic crown of sonnets;" fifteen linked sonnets in which the last line of one, slightly paraphrased, becomes the first line of the next, until the final entry combines the first lines of the preceding sonnets to become the fifteenth. Nelson explains her strict form as " . . . a kind of insulation, a way of protecting myself from the intense pain of the subject matter . . . I wrote this poem with my heart in my mouth and tears in my eyes."

From *A Wreath for Emmett Till*

A running boy, five men in close pursuit.
One dark, five pale faces in the moonlight.
Noise, silence, back–slaps. One match, five cigars.
Emmett Till's name still catches in the throat.

. . .

We can speak now, or bear unforgettable shame.
Rosemary for remembrance, Shakespeare wrote.
—*Marilyn Nelson*

2006 JOHN STEPTOE NEW TALENT AWARD

ADOFF, JAIME. *Jimi & Me.* Jump at the Sun/Hyperion Books for Children, 2005. Gr. 6–8.

Keith James, the narrator of Adoff's free-verse novel, is thirteen years old when his father, a music producer and fan of Jimi Hendrix, is shot by thugs during the robbery of a local deli. Keith escapes his feelings of loss by immersing himself in the music of his father's idol. Dad and Jimi were like Black hippie brothers who never knew each other. Shocked to find that her husband left them with huge debts, Keith's mother moves them from Brooklyn to a small, largely white Ohio town. Keith's loss is compounded by his mother's increasing withdrawal and prejudices he faces because of his biracial "caramel brown Frap-pu-ccino face—BIG, bushy 'fro." The revelation that Keith's father had another son named Jimi, three years older than Keith, was most distressing. "Everything is different now. / Even Hendrix songs don't sound the same, / all because of that name. / His voice reminding me of the pain."

Jimi confronts the possibility of reconciliation in the face of betrayal. Feeling as though his father has died a second time, Keith arranges to meet his half-brother.

Adoff's narrative captures Keith's anguish. The author's experience as a musician finds expression, not only in his description of music and the music business but also in the cadence of the book's language.

From *Jimi & Me*

two weeks
since I met Jimi and I'm tryin'
my best.
Some days it all makes sense.
Some days
it just hurts.
I feel hate towards dad,

but at least I know he tried.
He wasn't a bad guy.
He wasn't all good either.
But
he was my dad.
I try to keep telling myself that.
—*Jaime Adoff*

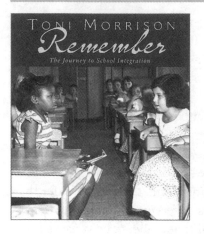

2005 WINNER

MORRISON, TONI. *Remember: The Journey to School Integration.* Illustrated with photographs. Houghton Mifflin, 2004. Gr. 6–8*

Archival photographs, strikingly reproduced in sepia tones, illustrate the era of school integration in Morrison's first historical work for young readers. Opening with images of segregated schools, the work documents the impact of the Supreme Court's decision that segregated educational facilities are "inherently unequal." It depicts integrated classrooms where southern schools complied with the ruling, the ugly resistance the decision too frequently evoked, and the brave children who faced vicious harassment to change our society. Later images show the wide-ranging effects of the decision as the movement spread to integrate restaurants, theaters, buses, and other public facilities. Throughout the book, Morrison reminds today's readers, "the path was not entered, the gate was not opened, the road was not taken only for those brave enough to walk it. It was for you as well. In every way, this is your story."

In the brief text accompanying the photographs, Morrison imagines thoughts that might have been in the minds of the young people in the various photographs. At the end of the book, thumbnail reproductions of the photographs expand the actual situation each records.

From *Remember*

Because remembering is the mind's first step toward understanding, this book is designed to take you on a journey through a time in American life when there was as much hate as there was love; as much anger as there was hope; as many heroes as cowards. —*Toni Morrison*

2005 HONORS

FLAKE, SHARON G. *Who Am I Without Him? Short Stories about Girls and the Boys in Their Lives.* Jump at the Sun/Hyperion Books for Children, 2004. Gr. 6–12.

Urban African American youth search for romance, friendship, and ultimately love as Flake's ten stories explore the roles boys and men play in the lives of girls. The titles of many of the stories reach out to capture the reader: "So I Ain't No Good Girl"; "The Ugly One"; "Don't Be Disrespecting Me"; "Wanted: A Thug." Respect, race, class, beauty, parental roles, and self-awareness are among the issues delivered in voices that capture the authentic lyric, cadence, and beat of contemporary Black teenspeak. The topics of these stories range from problem solving to humor, heartache, abuse, advice good and bad, crossing borders, and true love. It all adds up to a collection that reflects the variety of ways in which the African American youth of today see themselves.

From *Who Am I Without Him?*

People say things about me. Bad things. Momma says I give 'em reason to. That if I would just be a good girl—like the girls who wait for the bus with me in the mornings—then things wouldn't go so hard for me. But I don't wanna be like them girls: so plain and pitiful, boys don't even look their way or ask their names.

   I wanna be me. Ain't nothing wrong with that. Is it?
—*From "So I Ain't No Good Girl," Sharon G. Flake*

MOSES, SHELIA P. *The Legend of Buddy Bush.* Margaret K. McElderry, 2004. Gr. 6–9.

Uncle Buddy is family kin but not actual blood kin to twelve-year-old Pattie Mae. Pattie Mae admires him for his Harlem ways. She is glad to have him back when he returns to rural Rich Square, North Carolina. The story is set around a terrifying event that happened in 1947. Though fictionalized, it is an intimate account of an incident that made national news. Pattie Mae gradually begins to understand racism and the dangers that affected her family. Although she has observed many petty instances of unfairness, it rocks her when she witnesses the incident: an insulted white woman distorts an encounter into "attempted rape." Uncle Buddy is arrested and nearly lynched by members of the Ku Klux Klan.

Moses's writing style creates a narrative that veers between down-home folksy vernacular and an almost poetic cadence that often sings. In the intimacy of an imperfect family struggling to maintain their pride in a segregated world no matter what, the legend of Buddy Bush grows, revealing an endurance and resiliency that exact not only a heavy toll but also the admiration of more than just Pattie Mae.

From *The Legend of Buddy Bush*

Hey, baby, I'm fine. Ole Man Taylor let you off earlier today?"

"Yes, Grandma, he did."

"You wash up and get you someteat." I do as I'm told, and check on Grandpa, who is sleeping. My mind must be playing tricks on me because the sound I suddenly hear coming from the road is women folks singing. I rush to the front door and Lord I am in shock.

Sure enough, it is the women from church. The women from the choir.

All of them.

Walking.

Walking and singing.

"Jesus, what in the world is they doing?" Grandma says as she stands up.

They are all dressing in white and Miss Cora Mae Jones, who ain't related to us, is leading the choir.

"Hush, somebody calling my name," she sing on and on.

By the time they get to the doorstep, Grandma is singing, too. I join in as Grandma shouts for joy. —*Shelia P. Moses*

NELSON, MARILYN. *Fortune's Bones: The Manumission Requiem.* Front Street, 2004. Gr. 6–12*

In 1933, the skeletal remains of Fortune, an enslaved African American man who died in 1798, were donated to the Mattatuck Museum of Waterbury, Connecticut. Prior to 1996, the museum was unsure of the identity of the skeleton. It was later learned that Fortune and five members of his family were owned by Dr. Preserved Porter. It was determined that after Fortune's death, his bones were rendered and displayed by Dr. Porter and also used for anatomical study. With the discovery of new information about Dr. Porter and Fortune, the museum commissioned Nelson, poet laureate of Connecticut, to create a literary work to serve as part of a community healing. Conceived in the aftermath of the September 11, 2001, terrorist attack on the United States, this lyrical eulogy is based on Fortune's life, his family, the Porter family, and the Waterbury community. Nelson's six haunting poems (particularly haunting is the selection describing Fortune's wife having to dust his bones because Dr. Porter's wife feared to do so) are a requiem and a celebration of life and what may be thought of as Fortune's ultimate freedom.

From *Fortune's Bones*

Not My Bones
I was not this body,
I was not these bones.
This skeleton was just my
temporary home.
Elementary molecules converged for a breath,
then danced on beyond upon my individual death.
And I am not my body,
I am not my body.
—*Marilyn Nelson*

2005 JOHN STEPTOE NEW TALENT AWARD

HATHAWAY, BARBARA. *Missy Violet and Me.* Houghton Mifflin, 2004. Gr. 3–5.

Little does eleven-year-old Viney realize how much she will learn when she's sent to spend the summer with Missy Violet, Richmond County's prominent midwife. Her curiosity leads her to discover the mysterious contents of the midwifery medicine bag, and while assisting Missy Violet, she learns the rigors of "catching" a newborn baby. Her stubborn persistence leads to a heroic climax in this concise, fast-paced novel spiced with humor and built on well-researched facts.

From *Missy Violet and Me*

I'd handled myself like a big girl, like somebody with backbone. I wasn't the same silly little girl who thought babies came out of tree stumps and cabbage patches. I was a midwife's helper, and I knew a few things about "catchin" babies. —*Barbara Hathaway*

2004 WINNER

JOHNSON, ANGELA. *The First Part Last.*
Simon & Schuster Books for Young Readers,
2003. Gr. 6–12.

Feather is Bobby's baby daughter. The arrival of Bobby's baby daughter Feather means that at sixteen, he has to find a way to balance his own needs and those of his infant daughter in the absence of the baby's mother. Johnson's depiction of Bobby's situation reveals sadness and love as alternating chapters move between then and now. Only gradually (with well-paced tension) does the complex truth of Bobby's love for his girlfriend, Nia, the baby's mother, emerge. In a fluid writing style, where every single word contributes to the whole, and with an almost deceptive simplicity, Johnson creates a poignant, sometime humorous, always sensitive story of a young person who has to become a man sooner than expected. With quiet insistence, readers see a child become a parent, making a new life out of a loss and conquering pain and sorrow with a subtle essence of joy. The details of Bobby's daily struggle to balance many opposing forces result in a powerful portrayal of a sensitive and nurturing young man caught in a rare but realistic dilemma.

From *The First Part Last*

But I figure if the world were really right, humans would live life backward and for the first part last. They'd be all knowing in the beginning and innocent in the end. Then everyone could end their life on their momma or daddy's stomach in a warm room, waiting for the soft morning light. —*Angela Johnson*

2004 HONORS

DRAPER, SHARON M. *The Battle of Jericho.* Atheneum, 2003. Gr. 7–10.

High school junior Jericho Prescott is thrilled to receive an invitation to pledge for the Warriors of Distinction, his school's most prestigious service club, even when the pledging process seems unexpectedly demanding—a Warrior of Distinction is not afraid to lower himself for his brother, does not show fear, celebrates obedience, and never breaks the code of silence. For the first time, Jericho no longer feels like an outsider, and he has the attention of attractive, popular Arielle.

When the pledge masters demand that he miss a long-awaited music contest that could win him a scholarship to Juilliard, Jericho is ready to sacrifice his joy in playing the trumpet for acceptance by his peers. As the hazing rituals become increasingly disturbing, however, Jericho begins to question the price of belonging. Tragically, the hazing reaches its climax with the "Leap of Faith," as Jericho's beloved cousin, Josh, jumps to his death. Draper's engrossing, disturbing novel challenges young readers to think about how one measures self-worth and loyalty, and about the possibility of refusing to bow to peer pressure. The novel ends "as Josh did, in silence," but the issues it raises will continue to echo in the minds of its readers.

From *The Battle of Jericho*

> Jericho felt excited and anxious to begin whatever awaited. . . . He wasn't sure if he felt like curling into a ball and sleeping for a week, or exploding like a grenade and destroying something. All he knew was that whatever they asked him to do, he was ready to do it. —*Sharon M. Draper*

MCKISSACK, PATRICIA C., AND FREDRICK L. MCKISSACK. *Days of Jubilee: The End of Slavery in the United States.* Scholastic, 2003. Gr. 6–8*

The tumultuous period following the Civil War and the end of legal slavery for African Americans is the focus of this well-researched text. Using slave narratives as their primary source, the McKissacks have reconstructed the facts and stories of this critical period in American history. Showcased is the impact of events on the lives of real people, some as famous as Abraham Lincoln, others more obscure. The efforts the enslaved made to ensure their own freedom are an important part of this dramatic story. The authors address complicated issues such as the role of Blacks in the Confederate army. The readable text presents the difficulties of the times as well as the hopes and jubilation of the newly freed. Illustrations of the period and direct quotations from those involved provide a particular immediacy to the narrative. A time line, a bibliography, and an index are helpful additions.

From *Days of Jubilee*

Freedom meant different things to different people and they responded accordingly. For one woman, naming her child without her master's permission was freedom. Others felt freedom meant they could go wherever they wanted, whenever they wanted. Large groups of the freed migrated west and many men became cowboys, or signed on as Pullman car porters when the Transcontinental Railroad was completed. —*Patricia C. McKissack and Fredrick L. McKissack*

WOODSON, JACQUELINE. *Locomotion.* G. P. Putnam's Sons, 2003. Gr. 3–6.

In a novel of sixty poems, fifth-grader Lonnie Collins gradually reveals his grief and refinds his joy in living. The grief is the result of a tragic fire that four years earlier killed his loving parents. The fire also separated him from his dear sister Lili, who was adopted by a different family. The healing process begins with his caring foster mother and his teacher, Ms. Marcus, who introduces him to the beauty of poetry. The very process of writing in verse helps Lonnie to observe, think, mourn, remember, and finally to smile again. Set in contemporary Brooklyn, *Locomotion* is a lyrical yet realistic depiction of urban school life. In Woodson's capable hands, it is also a compelling and accessible story of a boy who can "write the word 'HOPE'" on his hand.

From *Locomotion*

Ms Marcus
says
line breaks help
us figure out
what matters
to the poet
Don't jumble your ideas
Ms Marcus says
Every line
should count
—*Jacqueline Woodson*

2004 JOHN STEPTOE NEW TALENT AWARD

SMITH, HOPE ANITA. *The Way a Door Closes.* Henry Holt, 2003. Gr. 3–5.

In this debut novel written in poetic prose, thirteen-year-old C.J. tells the poignant story of a family that learns to cope when the proud and recently unemployed father just walks out, closing the door behind him. In spite of neighborhood predictions that the father will never return, the youngster continues to hold on to the hope that his father will return. Thirty-four poems speak with a voice of pain, loss, the power of love, and ultimate triumph when the family is once again united.

From *The Way a Door Closes*

Schoolyard Sermon
My best friend, Preacher,
is being just that.
His sermon today is on fathers . . .
"Dads are light.
They have no roots.
One strong wind, and they're
gone . . .
History . . .
they don't come back." . . .
"My dad is coming back,"
I announce . . .
"Man," he says, "that only happens
once in a blue moon."
I smile as I head to my next class
and I say,
more to myself than to Preacher,
"But it happens."
—Hope Anita Smith

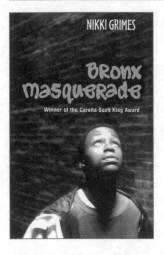

2003 WINNER

GRIMES, NIKKI. *Bronx Masquerade.* Dial, 2002. Gr. 6–8.

Bronx Masquerade is a masterful blend of poetry and prose. The result is a composite of the lives of contemporary teenagers taking on life in the twenty-first century. When Mr. Ward gives his racially mixed class the assignment to write a poem, the reader can almost hear the groans. Nonetheless, the resulting pieces give insight into the problems and concerns of the writers. Having a baby out of wedlock complicates Gloria's youthful journey; Raynard is dyslexic; Leslie is always angry until she learns that a fellow student, Porscha, is also struggling with the changes that come with the loss of a parent. The format attests to the power of poetry to succinctly express a wide range of thought and emotions.

From *Bronx Masquerade*

There's something about reading poetry. It's almost like acting . . . it's like you become somebody else and you can say anything, as long as it's a poem. Then, when you're finished, you just disappear into the dark and sit down, and you're back to being your own self. —*Nikki Grimes*

2003 HONORS

GRIMES, NIKKI. *Talkin' About Bessie: The Story of Aviator Elizabeth Coleman.* Illustrated by E. B. Lewis. Orchard, 2002. Gr. 2–5*

From the moment of her birth, Bessie's parents knew that she was someone special. Intellectually gifted, determined, and self-assured, Bessie Coleman became not only the first African American aviatrix but also an internationally known stunt pilot. She drew crowds of awestruck spectators to watch her daring performances. Written in lyrical prose, Coleman's life story unfolds in a series of vignettes, each from the perspective of a person with whom Bessie had some type of association. Her mother, though not formally educated, realized Bessie's abilities and made whatever sacrifices necessary to get her daughter an education.

Bessie went to France for flight training that she could not get as a "colored" person in America. This factually based fictional biography provides insight into Bessie's life and activities as a pilot, extending far beyond mere headline-grabbing performances. Bessie Coleman's achievements as an aviatrix and a stunt pilot are an orchestrated blend of words and illustrations.

From *Talkin' About Bessie*

Lord spoke kindly of the eagles and dove, but he also loved the raven: a strong mysterious black bird of high intelligence is she; a creature slighted by many, but cared for by God   that was Bessie. —*Nikki Grimes*

WOODS, BRENDA. *The Red Rose Box*. G. P. Putnam's Sons, 2002. Gr. 5–8.

Leah and her younger sister Ruth live in quiet Sulphur, Louisiana. They cannot imagine life thousands of miles away in California until their aunt Olivia sends train tickets for the girls to make the trip. The sisters find life in California much different from the segregated experiences they knew at home. Leah finds new opportunities so special that she cannot imagine anyone choosing to live in the Jim Crow South. When tragedy strikes the family, Leah and Ruth return to Los Angeles to make it their permanent home. Now the "wonderful" experiences are bittersweet, making Leah question if she can ever overcome the loss of her family. Perhaps the contents of the Red Rose Box may help. Brenda Woods's evocative novel successfully explores the complex emotions involved in leaving the past behind.

From *The Red Rose Box*

It felt like a million miles from Sulphur and crayfish, cotton fields and hand-me-down clothes, a one-room school house, segregation and Jim Crow. But I knew one thing. I knew that I would gladly give up this new comfort and freedom to be in my mama's arms, to feel the tenderness in my daddy's touch one more time. —*Brenda Woods*

2003 JOHN STEPTOE NEW TALENT AWARD

MCDONALD, JANET. *Chill Wind*. Frances Foster Books/Farrar Straus and Giroux, 2002. Gr. 7–12.

Bold and brash Aisha Ingram is a nineteen-year-old mother of two young children. A high school dropout with no plans for the future, she is at a crossroads for she has come to the end of the five-year limit on receiving public assistance. This "project girl" sees no future in the workfare option of cleaning graffiti from public spaces or in patrolling New York City's subway system as a member of a youth force. Who would have imagined that Aisha would have a golden opportunity to shine as a plus-size, roller-skating spokesmodel! BIGMODELS called, and the House of Rap 'n Roll, an urban roller rink, has Aisha in the house and on the payroll.

From *Chill Wind*

Raven's words came back again: "They kick you off welfare after five years." What was she going to do? With no diploma, no skills, and two kids, Aisha Ingram's chilled life had suddenly gotten a little too chilly. —*Janet McDonald*

2002 WINNER

TAYLOR, MILDRED D. *The Land.* Phyllis Fogelman Books/Penguin Putnam, 2001. Gr. 8–12.

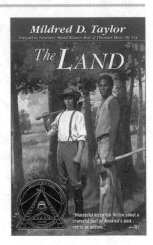

The Land chronicles the struggles and triumphs of Paul Edward Logan, the son of a white slave owner and an enslaved African Indian woman. Taylor offers a gripping and painful story of a young man's awakening to racial injustice. This riveting account takes place in Mississippi during Reconstruction and follows Paul Edward's growth to manhood. The unending injustices of that place and time, when race defined everything, are told through a narrative that is never whitewashed or turned into melodrama. Paul Edward's ability to cope is stretched to staggering degrees, but with the support of friends and through his own unending labor he makes his way toward the ultimate goal, a piece of land that represents paradise. A prequel to *Roll of Thunder, Hear My Cry* and other novels about the Logan family, this powerful family memoir is also a love story, a suspense thriller, and a meticulously detailed work of historical fiction. It is an unparalleled tour de force by one of children's literature's most prestigious writers.

From *The Land*

I watched him go, then sat down on a stump, closed my eyes and tried to take hold of my Fury. Ever since I had left my daddy's house, I had been learning and relearning that harsh lesson my daddy whipped into me when I was fourteen. It was a white man's world and I had to survive in it. —Mildred D. Taylor

2002 HONORS

FLAKE, SHARON G. *Money Hungry.* Jump at the Sun/Hyperion Books for Children, 2001. Gr. 6–8.

Thirteen-year-old Raspberry Hill is money hungry. She finds ways to make money to protect herself and her mother from being homeless again. She sells pencils and candy to her fellow students, washes cars, and cleans houses, stashing away the money she makes. She is determined to provide some sense of stability for her mother. Through a series of circumstances, life takes a downturn for Raspberry. She lends her friend Janae $200 of her hard-earned money without knowing why Janae needs it, her mother's application for housing under Section 8 is denied, and Janae's grandmother wrongfully accuses Raspberry of stealing her money. Then, frustrated by these events, Raspberry's mother throws Raspberry's stash out the window.

Raspberry's story involves characters like Odd Job, a man who washes cars at intersections, and invites the reader to reflect on such social issues as the effects of poverty, absentee parents, and one aspect of life in the projects. A real sense of community shines through the book, replete with believable people dealing with life's ups and downs and acknowledging the importance of friends and family.

From *Money Hungry*

Even now, Momma's always dreaming about the future. But you can't cash dreams in at the bank or buy bread or pay rent with 'em. You need hard cold cash for that. So every penny I get, I save. . . . Cause if you got money, people can't take stuff from you—not your house or your ride, not your family. They can't do nothing much to you, if you got a bankroll backing you up. —Sharon G. Flake

NELSON, MARILYN. *Carver: A Life in Poems.* Front Street, 2001. Gr. 6–9.

Marilyn Nelson's fifty-nine poems tell the life story of the famed scientist, inventor, musician, and artist George Washington Carver. Nelson tells the story through the voice of Carver and people who knew him. Susan Carver was a white woman who, with her husband, "owned" and raised young George. One poem is by a man sent by Carver's owner to find Carver and his mother after slave catchers had abducted them. There are selections from teachers in the schools where he studied, from his own students, from admirers, and even from detractors. The total gives a living picture of an admirable human being. Selections describe Carver's life from his birth to a slave woman in Diamond Grove, Missouri, and his childhood with Moses and Sam Carver, to his travels and work in parts of the Midwest, where he began his education. Poetic entries describe his life's work teaching at Tuskegee Institute and his continuing search for the many uses of the peanut and the sweet potato.

Handsome archival black-and-white photographs enhance the displayed text. Time-line notes at the bottom of selected pages place events in Carver's life within the context of world history.

From *Carver: A Life in Poems*

Four a.m. in the Woods
Darkness softens
tissue of mist between trees.
One by one the day's
unaccountable voices come out
like twilight fireflies, like stars.
The perceiving self sits
with his back against rough bark,
casting ten thousand questions into the future.
As shadows take shape, the curtains part
for the length of time it takes to gasp,
and behold, the purpose of his
life dawns on him.
—*Marilyn Nelson*

2001 WINNER

WOODSON, JACQUELINE. *Miracle's Boys.* G. P. Putnam's Sons, 2000. Gr. 6–10.

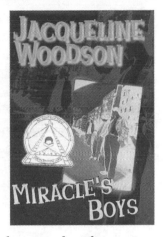

Miracle's Boys is the story of three brothers, Ty'ree, Charlie, and Lafayette, and their struggle to stay together as a family after the death of their mother. The family's struggles began two years earlier with the death of the father who drowned while saving a jogger and her dog who had fallen into an icy lake. Milagro, the boy's mother, worked hard to raise her boys. Although she could not give them many material things, she passed on her strong values and a love of learning.

Middle brother Charlie loses his way temporarily, has brushes with the law, deserts the family, associates with the wrong crowd, and ends up spending time in a juvenile facility. Ty'ree does not give up on Charlie, and the young prodigal eventually returns to the family unit. Youngest brother Lafayette comes to terms with Charlie's accusation that he caused his mother's death. Milagro, despite her death, proves to be a powerful presence in the lives of her sons—a presence felt throughout the entire narrative. The young men face hardships but demonstrate the resilience of the human spirit and the power of family love to help family members survive even the toughest circumstances.

From *Miracle's Boys*

Newcharlie moved the plastic bag away from his eyes so he could get a better look. He hadn't seen these pictures probably in years. I'd hidden them from him, afraid he'd burn them up too. But now I held them out so he could see, not afraid anymore. It was like the pictures were chiseled in my brain. "You tried to kill the memory of her," I said. "But she's too deep inside of us." —*Jacqueline Woodson*

2001 HONOR

PINKNEY, ANDREA DAVIS. *Let It Shine! Stories of Black Women Freedom Fighters.* Illustrated by Stephen Alcorn. Gulliver Books/Harcourt, 2000. Gr. 5–8*

Andrea Davis Pinkney offers brief, powerful portraits of ten African American women and their fight for freedom from sexism and oppression. Some of her subjects may not be familiar to young readers: Biddy Mason, Dorothy Irene Height, and Fannie Lou Hamer. Others, including Sojourner Truth, Harriet Tubman, and Rosa Parks, are better known. Pinkney's tellings, with their rich imagery and original, rhythmic, often colloquial language, bring fresh insights and perspectives. For example: "Sojourner traveled often on nothing more than her size-twelve feet throughout the United States preaching fairness and liberty." Jim Crow laws required Ida Wells-Barnett, as a Black woman, to ride in the smoking car during her weekly train trip. "Whew, that smoking car sure smelled nasty . . . The smoke was as thick as intolerance."

Each of these freedom fighters acted to improve the lives of all people. Colorful language and telling details, illustrated by Stephen Alcorn's stunning allegorical pictures, make up a beautiful and inspiring volume.

From *Let It Shine!*

Now, anybody knows that wishing and doing are two different things. And Mary McLeod Bethune wasn't just one of those sapheaded daydreamers. She was a doer. All she needed was a mustard seed of inspiration. —*Andrea Davis Pinkney*

2000 WINNER

CURTIS, CHRISTOPHER PAUL. *Bud, Not Buddy*. Delacorte, 1999. Gr. 4–6.

Christopher Paul Curtis's second novel, *Bud, Not Buddy*, is the first book to win both the Coretta Scott King Book Award and the Newbery Medal. It is the story of ten-year-old Bud Caldwell's quest to find his father. It is 1936, the height of the Great Depression. Bud's mother died four years earlier when he was just six years old. Running away from a cruel foster family, Bud carries in his cardboard suitcase fliers his mother had collected, advertising bass player Herman Calloway and the Dusky Devastators of the Great Depression. Buoyed by memories of his mother's love and his own "Rules and Things for Having a Funner Life and Making a Better Liar of Yourself," Bud sets out to find Calloway, whom he assumes to be his father.

On the way to finding the truth about his family, Bud encounters the kindness of strangers but also confronts the realities of Depression-era life. Soup kitchens, Hoovervilles and their wanton destruction by Pinkerton agents and police, labor strife, and racism make it dangerous for Bud to travel Michigan highways alone at night. Bud is a beguiling narrator, whose voice conveys his naive yet street-smart character.

From *Bud, Not Buddy*

Rules and Things Number 83: If a Adult Tells You Not to Worry, and You Weren't Worried Before, You Better Hurry and Start 'Cause You're Already Running Late. —*Christopher Paul Curtis*

2000 HONORS

ENGLISH, KAREN. *Francie.* Farrar Straus and Giroux, 1999. Gr. 7–10.

In a fast-paced story set in Alabama, Francie is the best student in her school. It is a time after World War II and before the turmoil of the Civil Rights Era. Francie and her mother work hard at the local Black boardinghouse as they wait for word from her father. He has gone to Chicago to work. When Francie is not working or attending school, she is reading. Her teacher recognizes her special skills and asks the young student to tutor sixteen-year-old Jesse, who has never learned to read well. The friendship that develops during the course of the tutoring causes Francie to make a difficult decision. Following a racial incident, Francie hides Jesse from the wrath of an unjust sheriff, placing her entire family in grave danger. Karen English has crafted a compelling story with a rich sense of tension, time, and space and well developed characters who truly come to life.

From *Francie*

By the time I had taken him through the sounds of the consonants so that he could remember them, I'd changed my mind. Jesse Pruitt wasn't no dummy and I was going to teach him to read. The idea gave me butterflies in my stomach. —*Karen English*

MCKISSACK, PATRICIA C., AND FREDRICK L. MCKISSACK. *Black Hands, White Sails: The Story of African-American Whalers.* Scholastic, 1999. Gr. 6–12.

The history of whaling in the Americas and around the globe is an exciting and captivating story of strong, fearless, ruthless, and often lawless men. This account of the roles that African American sailors played in the whaling industry is interspersed with information about the risks and rigors of life aboard ship.

"Southern whalers and others with an aversion to living and working with black sailors" soon learned that when hurricane winds were blowing or their boat was attached to a raging sperm whale, it didn't matter what color the hands were that handled the sails or pulled the oars. All men had to work together if they were to survive. This reality earned Blacks respect, or at least tolerance, even though they were not always accepted.

Short, readable chapters present basic information about ships, whales, and whaling. *Black Hands, White Sails* chronicles the lives and deeds of Black sea captains and whalers, along with the more commonly known adventures of white seamen. The parts played by the abolitionist Frederick Douglass and the ingenious Paul Cuffe, along with photographs, diary entries, traditional sea shanties, folk sayings, and superstitions, make *Black Hands, White Sails* a fascinating reading experience for all ages.

MYERS, WALTER DEAN. *Monster.* HarperCollins, 1999. Gr. 9–12.

How does an ordinary kid, an OK student with a developing interest in film, living with two parents struggling to raise two sons in an urban community, find himself jailed and labeled as another of those "monsters from the ghetto"? He is, after all, only a kid who most of the time focuses on ways of using film to document his surroundings and on negotiating to coexist with ever more demanding street gangs.

Myers's book takes the form of a film script written by the main character, Steve Harmon, who uses it to calm the fear he is experiencing. Jailed as an accomplice to murder, Steve diverts his anxiety by analyzing the situation as an outsider. The story unfolds with short filmmaker's instructions: cut to/long shot/close-up, seamlessly intertwined with the story of a real robbery and murder committed by local gang members.

The reader is never quite sure which of the adults in Steve's world, including his defense attorney, believe and support his plea of innocence. He receives unwavering support only from his mother.

The central character tells his story from a third-person perspective, as if he were an arm's-length observer. The realities of the justice system put a face on crime that juxtaposes the vagaries of honesty and integrity among thieves.

1999 WINNER

JOHNSON, ANGELA. *Heaven.* Simon & Schuster Books for Young Readers, 1998. Gr. 6–10.

Fourteen-year-old Marley is living a happy life in the small town of Heaven, Ohio, surrounded by family and friends in an almost idyllic community enjoying a connection to the outside world through letters from her uncle Jack. Then, quite by accident, Marley learns that her parents are really her aunt and uncle, that "Uncle Jack" is really her father, and that her mother died when she was a baby. Shattered by this discovery, Marley closes herself off from family love and begins to question every belief she had previously valued. As Marley sees it, only the wide-open spaces, the farmland and the fields, seem unchanged by what she has learned—and it is in those open spaces that she seeks comfort. Eventually Marley understands that all families have secrets that she can accept truths about herself and that real "heaven" is where love is unwavering and unconditional. Johnson's compelling first-person narrative is a finely tuned vehicle for an engaging protagonist who speaks with candor.

1999 HONORS

GRIMES, NIKKI. *Jazmin's Notebook.* Dial, 1998. Gr. 9–12.

Jazmin Shelby is a bright, inquisitive fourteen-year-old who writes her feelings and observations in a journal that provides special insight to readers of this novel. Jazmin is a girl who had a strong family beginning that has since come apart. Her father, now dead, insisted on the z in the spelling of her name to reflect his love for jazz. Her mother is in the hospital, suffering from a mental illness. As the story opens Jazmin finally has a home with her older sister, CeCe. She goes through the normal teenage anxieties: worries about her appearance and fears about the future. She also handles attraction to a handsome boy who takes her interest as an invitation to rape. Most troubling of all, however, is her inability to accept her mother's illness and limitations. Jazmin's writing and her growing maturity finally give her the courage to visit her mother in the hospital, where she gains new hope from the changes she can observe.

A stunning combination of poetry and prose brings a special dimension to this coming-of-age novel. It is written with a sense of humor and a texture that will engage its readers.

HANSEN, JOYCE, AND GARY MCGOWAN. *Breaking Ground, Breaking Silence: The Story of New York's African Burial Ground.* Henry Holt, 1998. Gr. 8–12*

In 1991, the African Burial Ground in New York City was rediscovered, offering scholars and ultimately everyone a unique look at the lives of Blacks in one section of colonial America. This volume offers young people a compelling look at the work of anthropologists, historians, and scholars as they piece together the elements of this long-hidden history. The authors use the physical evidence, documents, and narratives of the time to complete as much of the picture as is currently possible.

The combined talents of a team that brought scholarly research skills, an archaeological background, and outstanding writing abilities to the project have produced a historically accurate and readable text. In words and pictures, Joyce Hansen and Gary McGowan describe social conditions, ancestral traditions, and types of personal effects gleaned from the study of the remains of African Americans in a volume that closes yet another gap in the history of Blacks in America.

JOHNSON, ANGELA. *The Other Side: Shorter Poems.* Orchard, 1998. Gr. 7–12*

When writer Angela Johnson received word from her grandmother that Shorter, Alabama, was about to be razed to make room for a dog track, she made a literal and mental pilgrimage there. The result is this captivating collection of poems. Life in the small town of Shorter is crisply described by these concise pieces with a biographical overtone. Each poem stands on its own, but together they are evocative of another time with a clear sense of place and community. Johnson does not sentimentalize the past; rather, she celebrates the people who created families and communities despite the difficulties of the times. The realities of life in the rural South are never glossed over. The emotional tone of the poems varies from pathos to humor, reflecting the author's early life and coming of age in a loving, supportive community.

Through clever use of language, Johnson paints vivid pictures that allow readers to share her love and affection for her family and their small-town life. Family photographs add a further connection for readers.

1999 JOHN STEPTOE NEW TALENT AWARD

FLAKE, SHARON G. *The Skin I'm In.* Jump at the Sun/Hyperion Books for Children, 1998. Gr. 9–12.

Maleeka Madison begins seventh grade determined to fit in. Her classmates tease her relentlessly about her physical appearance, particularly her homemade clothes and dark skin. She decides to become part of the inner circle of Charlese, "the baddest thing in this school." She endures cruel treatment from Charlese and her friends, still believing that is better than to be without friends. When she sees her new English teacher, Miss Saunders, she is shocked at her face, which "looks like someone threw a hot pot of something on it." Nonetheless, Miss Saunders appears confident and unruffled by the students' reactions. Miss Saunders recognizes a kindred spirit in Maleeka and encourages her writing skills even as Maleeka attempts to hide her strong academic abilities.

Flake has produced a thoughtful and timely story that explores peer pressure as well as the role that color plays in the body image of African American teens. Maleeka is a strong protagonist, struggling to become comfortable with who she is. The voices of the characters ring true and school and community reflect authenticity.

1998 WINNER

DRAPER, SHARON M. *Forged by Fire.* Atheneum, 1997. Gr. 7–10.

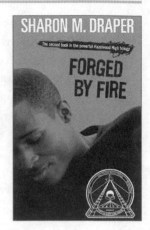

Forged by Fire is a contemporary novel that unflinchingly comes to grips with many of the problems that beset the youth of today's society—broken homes, drugs, and child abuse—problems that are so much a part of a dysfunctional family.

 Teenaged Gerald, whom some readers met in *Tears of a Tiger*, learns early in his troubled life that he must grow beyond his years if he is to survive and protect his younger sister, Angel. Gerald's and Angel's lives are stalked by tragedy: the death of Aunt Queen, the one person who truly showed them love; life with a substance-abusing and seemingly unaware mother; and the cruel acts of Jordan, their mother's boyfriend. Gerald finally takes matters into his own hands when he finds that Jordan is sexually molesting Angel. For some readers, the raging fire that brings Jordan to a tragic, but not entirely regrettable, end and nearly costs Angel her life may seem symbolic of the fire that rages in Gerald's spirit. It is the fire that in the end forges together this fragile family.

1998 HONORS

HANSEN, JOYCE. *I Thought My Soul Would Rise and Fly: The Diary of Patsy, a Freed Girl.* Scholastic, 1997. Gr. 4–8.

Twelve-year-old Patsy, a slave in the Davis household in Mars Bluff, South Carolina, learns to read and write and secretly keeps a diary of the day-to-day occurrences in the "master's" family and the family of slaves he holds in bondage. Through her diary entries, individual personalities come alive: the slave Nancy, who claimed that "Missus was training her to be a fine ladies maid, not a cook"; Reverend McNeal, who started the organization that "helps men and women learn about government and voting"; the field hands, who fertilize the cotton fields with pine straw for the new planting next year; and Patsy herself, who reads from Goody Two Shoes and secretly passes her knowledge of words and letters to the other slaves. Patsy's diary dramatically reveals the trials, tribulations, quandaries, and uncertainties that ensued for the freed slaves after the Emancipation Proclamation. She also presents the changes the proclamation produced in the lives of the "masters" and "mistresses," whose indolence and dependency on others' labors were uprooted, and makes poignantly evident their lack of survival skills.

HASKINS, JAMES. *Bayard Rustin: Behind the Scenes of the Civil Rights Movement.* Hyperion Books for Children, 1997. Gr. 5–8*

Bayard Rustin, born in 1912, was a civil rights activist and organizer whose pacifist beliefs and commitment to the principles of nonviolent action inspired Martin Luther King Jr.

Raised by his grandparents in Pennsylvania, Rustin maintained that his Quaker grandmother was the greatest influence on his life. Citing an extensive bibliography, including primary source material, Haskins integrates the story of the Civil Rights Movement in the United States with details of Rustin's personal and professional life. Quotations address incidents from Rustin's childhood and young adulthood, showing the development of his beliefs and commitment to issues of peace, equality, and justice.

Although Rustin served time in prison for refusing to join the military during World War II, had been a member of the Young Communist League, and was openly homosexual, his beliefs and organizational skills made him a dynamic leader in the Civil Rights Movement. His talent in that area was most powerfully effective as he planned the procedures for the 1963 March on Washington, which led to the passage of the Civil Rights Act of 1964. Haskins creates an inspirational portrait of a man who left a lasting legacy in the struggle for equality and justice in the United States and throughout the world.

1997 WINNER

MYERS, WALTER DEAN. *Slam!* Scholastic, 1996. Gr. 6–8.

From preschool through high school, both off and on the basketball court, Harlem-born Ice and Slam have been friends. Now seventeen-year-old Greg "Slam" Harris has transferred to a Bronx high school specializing in the arts. Both young men have NBA dreams and aspirations. Slam discovers that the students at his new school are serious young artists, and it becomes apparent that he must work hard to achieve good grades and personal satisfaction. It is also apparent that the basketball team, the perennially losing Panthers, could use a star player. What the Panthers don't need is a star with an attitude, especially one who is in continual conflict with the coach. In one school year, Slam and Ice take separate paths. Slam embraces athletic and academic excellence while Ice accepts cash for drugs.

Myers's fast-paced novel develops a vivid flesh-and-blood portrait of young people in the Harlem community. For basketball fans, the description of moves on the court is hard to beat.

1997 HONOR

MCKISSACK, PATRICIA C., AND FREDRICK L. MCKISSACK. *Rebels Against Slavery: American Slave Revolts.* Scholastic, 1996. Gr. 9–12*

Patricia and Fredrick McKissack have written a most compelling narrative of those who resisted slavery in the Americas. *Rebels Against Slavery* includes the stories of individuals who bravely rebelled, runaway slaves who formed maroon communities, leaders who organized insurrections, conductors on the Underground Railroad, and those who became eloquent exponents of abolition. While the authors describe the contributions of all who fought slavery, their work emphasizes the role of African Americans. As the escaped slave and abolitionist Henry Garnet noted, "Others may be our allies, but the battle is ours." In these pages, the courage of slavery's opponents is brought to life. This book brings memories of a past that helped to map the future to a new generation. The authors stated,

> As rebels for a righteous cause, they should be remembered for the terrible risks they knowingly took, the extraordinary determination they displayed and the important role they played in the abolition of slavery.

1997 JOHN STEPTOE NEW TALENT AWARD

SOUTHGATE, MARTHA. *Another Way to Dance.* Delacorte, 1996. Gr. 9–12.

Fourteen-year-old Vicki Harris imagines that someday she will have an opportunity to meet the dancer of her dreams, Mikhail Baryshnikov. This young ballerina is his greatest fan. She says, "I love him more than anything in the world." When Vicki is accepted into the prestigious summer program of the New York School of American Ballet, she is thrilled and frightened. The competition and racial tensions are easier to bear with her newfound friend and classmate, Stacey, the only other African American enrolled that summer. Summer also brings romance. Michael of Harlem may not be Mikhail of Latvia, but he, too, has dreams beyond those of flipping burgers. With New York City and the love of ballet as backdrops, Southgate gives a vivid picture of a thoughtful and talented young woman coming to terms with class, race, and cultural differences. She learns indeed that beyond the world of ballet, there is "another way to dance."

1996 WINNER

HAMILTON, VIRGINIA. *Her Stories: African American Folktales, Fairy Tales, and True Tales.* Illustrated by Leo Dillon and Diane Dillon. Scholastic, 1995. Gr. 6–8.

In this aesthetically attractive volume, Virginia Hamilton has gathered a collection of stories from African American culture in genres to fit just about everyone's literary tastes and has adapted them to her own inimitable "telling voice." As the title implies, the stories focus on African American women's stories. Notes at the end of each tale provide information on background, origin, and authenticity or historical significance. The repertoire includes familiar "girls and animals" stories such as "Little Girl and Buh Rabby" and one perhaps less familiar but thematically popular in many cultures, "Marie and Redfish." Fairy tales recall European and Asian versions of "Cinderella" and "The Talking Eggs." Readers will find that Hamilton's supernatural tales really do abound with "weird, mystical and magical elements . . . and odd and eerie events in the lives of female subjects." The true tales are touching biographical sketches of courageous women whose life stories were gleaned from documents collected under government projects in the 1920s and 1930s. In their carefully detailed illustrations, master artists Leo and Diane Dillon have captured the nuances of each story—from humorous to frightening to somber. *Her Stories* is a book to savor and to share.

1996 HONORS

CURTIS, CHRISTOPHER PAUL. *The Watsons Go to Birmingham—1963.*
Delacorte, 1995. Gr. 6–8.

Ten-year-old Kenny Watson narrates this funny and touching story of his
family, "The Weird Watsons" of Flint, Michigan, as they are sometimes
called. He relates comic stories of the escapades of his older brother, Byron,
and the efforts of his strict but loving parents to keep the boys and their
little sister, Joetta, out of trouble. Before long, however, Byron's pranks
become more troubling, prompting Mom and Dad to plan a trip to Grandma's in Birmingham, Alabama. Here, the story subtly shifts gears. As the
family travels farther south, they find themselves headed for a place and
time in history that will change them—and the country—forever: the Civil
Rights Movement.

Christopher Paul Curtis does a masterful job of weaving comedy and
tragedy in this impressive first novel. He creates memorable and realistic
characters that engage the reader from beginning to end. The author man-
ages to present both a warm family story and a tragic episode of history in
a style that makes both themes clear to the reader.

WILLIAMS-GARCIA, RITA. *Like Sisters on the Home Front.* Dutton, 1995.
Gr. 8–12.

Gayle Whitaker is fourteen and pregnant, again. This time her mother
escorts her to a women's clinic where she undergoes an abortion. The tough-
talking Gayle is frightened. Mama is fed up and at the end of her rope. Drawing upon an African American tradition, Mama sends Gayle and her toddler
son, Jose, down south to spend time with her minister uncle, his wife, and
their daughter, the straight-laced cousin Cookie. In their quiet, antebellum
home, the former site of a slaveholding plantation, Gayle meets the family
matriarch, Great. This stately, near-death grandmother has a special fond-
ness for the somewhat wayward and ignorant girl. Great sees in Gayle her
own teenage behavior. It is Great who tells Gayle stories of the past that
help Gayle to see that she indeed has a future.

Gayle appeared as a minor character in Williams-Garcia's first novel, *Blue
Tights.* In this, her third novel, the author continues her compassionate and

humorous portraits of New York City teenagers with flawed characters who are given opportunities for tremendous growth.

WOODSON, JACQUELINE. *From the Notebooks of Melanin Sun.* Scholastic, 1995. Gr. 9–12.

Thirteen-year-old Melanin Sun and his mother are extremely close. His name reflected their special bond: Melanin because that is what made him dark, and Sun because "his mom could see the sun shining through him." Things change between the two of them during the summer of Melanin's thirteenth year. Suddenly his mama has a new friend—a white woman named Kristin. Before too long his mother admits that Kristin is more than a friend—they are lovers. Just when Melanin is coming to grips with his own sexual feelings, he must sort out new feelings toward his mother. For a while, it appears that the new truth about his mother will destroy their special relationship. Melanin lashes out at Mama, but despite his confusion, he needs her in his life and tries to make some connection with Kristin.

Jacqueline Woodson presents a powerful, trailblazing story, reaching across barriers of race and sexual orientation. She has created a strong, honest character in Melanin Sun, whose first-person narrative draws the reader into his innermost thoughts.

1995 WINNER

MCKISSACK, PATRICIA C., AND FREDRICK L. MCKISSACK. *Christmas in the Big House, Christmas in the Quarters.* Illustrated by John Thompson. Scholastic, 1994. Gr. 3–5.

The lives of slaves who work the Virginia plantation contrasts with the lives of the plantation owner and his family at Christmastime. In a story set during the last Christmas before the Civil War, the book presents images of traditions, superstitions, religious observances, songs, holiday menus, and games. The authors show the contrast between the gifts and decorations easily available to the master's family and those of the slaves, who ingeniously made their decorations from nature's bounty.

Rumblings of unrest filter through the activities in the big house, and in the quarters there are secretive discussions among the slaves from neighboring plantations who were given passes for a short family reunion. The book closes with a portentous message:

> The way talk goin' I got a feeling we aine gon' need to run away. One day soon we gon' celebrate the Big Times in freedom.

John Thompson's dramatic paintings, the authors' historical notes, and a useful bibliography further enrich this moving story.

1995 HONORS

HANSEN, JOYCE. *The Captive.* Scholastic, 1994. Gr. 9–12.

Through the voice of a master storyteller, twelve-year-old Kofi, the son of an African king, describes the way a joyful Ashanti celebration turns with unbelievable swiftness into a scene of treachery, murder, capture, and slavery.

"I became a captive. . . . I had lost my home, my family and even myself. I was a slave dressed in filthy loincloth. I could hardly remember what my beautiful robe looked like."

The narration covers the horrors of the slave ship, the indignity of the slave auction market, the rigorous work assigned to the young slaves, the strange and reserved relationship Kofi observes between his "master" and the master's wife.

Over time, Kofi masters the English language and has an encounter with the African American seaman Paul Cuffe. Eventually, as a freedman, Kofi visits Sierra Leone, marries his early love, Ama, and raises his family in America. The well-researched novel closes on this rich promise:

"I made a decision that I too [like his father, Kwame, and Paul Cuffe] would fight against slavery and open my heart and home to unfortunate men and women in bondage. . . . The trial of my life had not been in vain."

MCKISSACK, PATRICIA C., AND FREDRICK MCKISSACK JR. *Black Diamond: The Story of the Negro Baseball Leagues.* Scholastic, 1994. Gr. 8–12*

This carefully researched volume tells the story of the Negro baseball leagues and dispels early myths about the "all-American" game. As early as 1845, there were organized guidelines for playing. They played their first all-star game before the Civil War.

The history covers individual players, such as Satchel Paige; Moses Fleetwood Walker, who played for the American Association in Toledo, Ohio; and Sol White, an amateur ballplayer and writer from whose records much history was learned. White, chronicled the history of the Cuban Giants (1887), the first professional all-Black team, because of their team name, were able to play against white teams. White writes, "not one of them was white nor could they speak a word of Spanish," but calling themselves Cuban opened the door.

The hardships the players endured were legendary—the lack of eating or sleeping facilities on the road, the unwritten requirement that they often play the clown to draw fans to the games, and financial inequities—any one of which could have been a deterrent if not for the players' deep love of the game. Profiles of many players, some of whom made the major leagues: include Satchel Paige, Roy Campanella, and Jackie Robinson. The Cooperstown Baseball Hall of Fame finally included Black players after years of rejection. An annotated player roster provides an overview of the many personalities who sacrificed so much for a game they loved.

WOODSON, JACQUELINE. *I Hadn't Meant to Tell You This.* Delacorte, 1994. Gr. 5–9.

Despite differences of race and class, Marie and Lena ignore the taunts of schoolmates and become best friends. Although Marie, from a middle-class African American family, seems to have little in common with poor, white Lena, the girls share a bond that means more than their differences: both girls have lost their mothers. As they share their deepest and most personal secrets, Marie is faced with a dilemma that can often confront good friends: can she help Lena more by betraying her confidence or should she keep her promise and remain silent?

Woodson's sensitive and skillful telling of this story places important issues before the reader: friendship across races, class differences, peer pressure, and family secrets. Woodson presents no easy answers but rather an honest portrait of the importance of seeking and finding understanding in all kinds of people.

1995 GENESIS AWARD
(later the JOHN STEPTOE AWARD FOR NEW TALENT)

DRAPER, SHARON M. *Tears of a Tiger.* Atheneum, 1994. Gr. 9–12.

The opening words of this page-turner pull the reader into a gripping story of friendship, irrevocable injury, and death—a relentless story rife with contemporary reality.

A newspaper headline screams:
Teen Basketball Star Killed in Fiery Crash

Andrew Jackson, the driver of the car and Robert Washington's best friend, finds his life forever changed by this avoidable accident. He closes himself off from a solicitous family, walks dazedly through school and studies, and avoids what seems to be useless help from a psychiatrist. Draper takes the reader into the heart and soul of everyone touched by this tragedy: B. J. Carson, who did not drink but feels guilty because he did not try to stop the others on that fateful night; Keisha, the love interest who worries about Andy's depression; and Andy's little brother Monty, who does not understand Andy's screaming nightmares. Each person works through the tragedy to the very uncompromising conclusion when Andy, unable to forgive or forget, takes his own life. Powerful words and powerful questions are the benchmarks of this hard-hitting young adult novel. One can almost understand Andy's decision after reading his poetry.

1994 WINNER

JOHNSON, ANGELA. *Toning the Sweep.* Orchard, 1993. Gr. 6–8.

Toning the Sweep, a cross-generational story, celebrates Grandma Ola's life even as that life, ravaged by cancer, is quietly slipping away. Fourteen-year-old Emily and her mother have come to help Ola pack, bid farewell to her beloved desert, and move to spend the rest of her life with family in Cleveland.

Using a camcorder, Emily videotapes Ola with each of her friends. She makes a memory of their tragedies, dreams, and hopes so many times gone unfulfilled. The camera records the reason for her mother's quiet anger against the Ola whom Emily loves and brings a stronger understanding to their mother-daughter relationship. As Emily listens to Ruth and David and to Aunt Martha and all the other aunts, she becomes aware of the philosophical approach to life that makes them as relentlessly enduring as the Arizona desert they call home. Emily includes lizards, plants, and trees that are the natural background of this arid place.

Readers will be intrigued to learn the poignant meaning of toning the sweep and its significance in the lives of Emily and her mother.

1994 HONORS

MYERS, WALTER DEAN. *Malcolm X: By Any Means Necessary.* Illustrated with black and white photographs. Scholastic, 1993. Gr. 6–12*

Malcolm X's quiet confrontation with police in Harlem introduces the life of a man who left an indelible mark on contemporary American history. His poverty-stricken childhood deteriorated further after the death of his father and his mother's slow and tragic mental breakdown. In his youth, Malcolm often used his academic prowess and brilliant mind to make a flashy but less than savory living which eventually landed him in prison. Six years of imprisonment introduced him to the principles and philosophy of Islam—a turning point in the life of the man who became Malcolm X. The X signifies the eradication of the surname a slave received, symbolic of the irrevocable loss of the name given in Africa.

Sidelights of African American history reveal the development of Malcolm X's personality, including the Marcus Garvey movement, the heroic work of the 54th Massachusetts Regiment of Civil War fame, the Anthony Burns slave case, and Malcolm X's interaction with Fidel Castro.

Malcolm X's thinking evolves from total hatred of the white man to the realization that there is wisdom in being willing to accept people as individuals.

Myers's skillful writing makes the life of Malcolm X accessible to young adult readers. The book includes a bibliography covering the early 1930s to the present.

THOMAS, JOYCE CAROL. *Brown Honey in Broomwheat Tea.* Illustrated by Floyd Cooper. HarperCollins, 1993. Gr. 3–6.

The poems in this outstanding collection speak in many voices: a plea for acceptance in "Cherish Me"; cautionary wariness in the title piece, "Brown Honey in Broomwheat Tea"; and the strength that is an integral part of African American heritage in "Becoming the Tea."

> But like the steeping brew
> The longer I stand
> The stronger I stay.

Thomas's rhythmic patterns, image-filled language, and provocative themes evoke a wide range of emotions. Although perhaps particularly attuned to the African American heritage, the ideas are worthy of contemplation and reflection by readers regardless of their ethnic heritage.

1993 WINNER

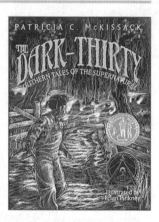

MCKISSACK, PATRICIA C. *The Dark-Thirty: Southern Tales of the Supernatural.* Illustrated by Brian Pinkney. Knopf, 1992. Gr. 6–8.

Patricia McKissack has written a collection of stories made for reading aloud or for telling "at that special time when it is neither day nor night and when shapes and shadows play tricks on the mind." There is a well-balanced mix of the humorous, the ghostly, and the supernatural among the ten entries. Readers will probably make individual choices among stories such as that of the Pullman porter who tried to avoid the 11:59, known as the death train, but answered its call on a gloomy night, and that of the slave who took a lesson from the wasps in making a wise decision to disobey his master. Or perhaps they will join in the fun of mastering the monster in the tale of the chicken coop. Each story is introduced with a historical note giving its foundation or origin. Brian Pinkney's scratchboard illustrations are a fitting complement to the mood of the stories.

1993 HONORS

MCKISSACK, PATRICIA C., AND FREDRICK L. MCKISSACK. *Sojourner Truth: Ain't I a Woman?* Scholastic, 1992. Gr. 5–8*

The McKissacks's stirring biography has captured the strength, the steadfastness, and the perseverance of a powerful woman determined to be free.

Details of Sojourner Truth's efforts provide insights into her struggles to keep her family together, save the life of her wayward son, and escape from the deceit of two religious charlatans. Meticulous research documents Sojourner Truth's life as she traveled speaking against slavery and fighting for all women's rights. In a slavery dispute, Sojourner Truth was the first Black woman to defeat a white man in a court of law. There was rapt attention when this imposing figure, over six feet tall, spoke with moving dignity. In answer to a minister's charge that God had intended women to be subservient because they were indeed the weaker sex, Truth responded:

"I have ploughed and I have planted. And I have gathered into barns, and no man could head me . . . I have borne children and seen them sold into slavery when I cried out in a mother's grief none heard me but Jesus—and ain't I a woman."

The McKissacks's biography is enriched with photographs and a section of biographical sketches of personalities, white and Black, who were a part of Sojourner Truth's memorable life.

MYERS, WALTER DEAN. *Somewhere in the Darkness.* Scholastic, 1992. Gr. 7–12.

Somewhere in the darkness a father is trying to establish a relationship between himself and the son he abandoned at an early age. On a dark night, Crab, just escaped from prison, shows up at his teenage son's home. He abruptly tells guardian Mama Jean that he has come to claim his son. With this, Crab and Jimmy begin a cross country trek during which Jimmy learns who his father is—an escapee, a con man, a womanizer, but still a man who wants to be a father to his son. Just before Crab's death, there is reconciliation and the poignancy of the moment when Jimmy realizes he has learned from Crab the kind of father he himself wants to be.

"Jimmy thought about his having a child. He would tell him all the secrets he knew, looking right into his eyes and telling him nothing but the truth.

That way there would be a connection . . . something that would be there even when they weren't together. He would know . . . where their souls touched and where they didn't."

Somewhere in the Darkness speaks to all who are parents and to those who someday will be.

WALTER, MILDRED PITTS. *Mississippi Challenge.* Bradbury, 1992. Gr. 7–12*

Mississippi Challenge is a documented study of a state whose historical treatment of African Americans is memorable for its cruelty and inhumanity. With candor, Walter traces freedom movements past and present and details the triumphs and failures of citizens who fought and died for justice: the sit-ins of the 1960s, the often fatal attempts at voter registration, and the inequalities in educational expenditures, which fostered the establishment of the freedom schools.

Blended into the text on contemporary affairs is a careful study of the early history of the state, the lives of some of the leaders, and little-known facts about nineteenth-century African American political leaders. This material helps youthful readers to link the past with the present.

Black-and-white photographs and personal interviews extend the information in this historically based reference. A scholarly bibliography provides reference sources for further research.

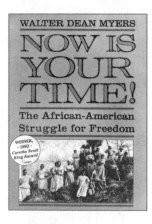

1992 WINNER

MYERS, WALTER DEAN. *Now Is Your Time! The African American Struggle for Freedom.* HarperCollins, 1991. Gr. 4–8*

In his first nonfiction book, Walter Dean Myers relates a memorable history of African Americans that spans over four centuries. The opening chapters share an aspect of African history often omitted from history texts—the time of high culture, noble rulers, great centers of learning, and scholars.

Scholarly research, including interviews with descendants of those captured, and carefully selected photographs from historical collections are the foundation of a book that eloquently tells the story of African Americans who achieved in spite of hardships. Myers's prose is moving and convincing:

> I claim the darkest moments of my people and celebrate their perseverance. I claim the joy and the light and the music and the genius and the muscle and the glory of these I write about . . . and of the legions who have passed this way without yet having their stories told.

1992 HONOR

GREENFIELD, ELOISE. *Night on Neighborhood Street.* Illustrated by Jan Spivey Gilchrist. Dial, 1991. Gr. K–3.

From dusk to deep into the night, these seventeen poems celebrate life in the neighborhood at that special time when the workday is done. Sleepovers, crying babies, church meetings, "Fambly Time," the child fearful of the dark, and kids playing on the street corner are all depicted. Gouache paintings highlighted with pastels accompany the poetry. Greenfield recognizes the many temptations toward wrongdoing that often accompany nighttime yet shows that the community can cope by uniting and offering "warmth and life" to undo the attractions of "The Seller" and others who want to harm its inhabitants. Powerful words offer comfort and solace to children with rhythms and images that soften the darkness's ability to frighten. Night becomes friend instead of nightmare.

1991 WINNER

TAYLOR, MILDRED D. *The Road to Memphis.* Dial, 1990. Gr. 6–8.

Cassie Logan's personal courage serves her well during a dangerous trip she makes from Mississippi to Tennessee in 1941 with her brother Stacey and his friends in Stacey's new car. Out on the open highway, the four African American teenagers, far from the protection of their families and their community, face unknown hazards at every turn in the road. This gripping narrative re-creates the perilous tensions of that time and place, as Cassie crosses over an invisible boundary and suddenly finds herself traveling into the unfamiliar terrain of adulthood.

1991 HONORS

HASKINS, JAMES. *Black Dance in America: A History through Its People.* Illustrated with photographs. HarperCollins, 1990. Gr. 6–12*

Brief biographical passages about individual African American dancers are chronologically arranged and connected by descriptions of the dances they invented or refined, providing an accessible overview of this distinctive art form. Haskins also provides a social and historical context by showing the ways Black dance influenced and was influenced by dance in general.

JOHNSON, ANGELA. *When I Am Old with You.* Illustrated by David Soman. Orchard, 1990. Gr. Pre-K–2.

In this warm, cross-generational story, the reader meets a child and his grandfather sharing hours of comfortable enjoyment. As they play cards, go fishing, enjoy a quiet picnic, or meet with friends at a lively party, the little boy muses that these are the things they will do together when he is as old as his grandfather. There is a moment of nostalgic sadness when the two are looking at the family album and each sheds tears for a different reason. One of the most endearing lines in the book occurs when the little boy, totally unaware of age differences, reflects on the idea that when he is old with his grandfather, they will sit, each in his own rocking chair, and "just talk about things." In word and picture, *When I Am Old with You* speaks with simple eloquence of the innocence of childhood.

1990 WINNER

MCKISSACK, PATRICIA C., AND FREDRICK L. MCKISSACK. *A Long Hard Journey: The Story of the Pullman Porter.* Illustrated with photographs. Walker, 1989. Gr. 6–8*

The authors combined in-depth research from primary and secondary sources to provide an uncompromising account of the history of African

Americans who worked as porters aboard George Pullman's luxury sleeping cars. Whereas the first generation of porters were newly freed from enslavement and grateful for work, poor working conditions and mistreatment at the hands of management led succeeding generations to unite under the leadership of A. Philip Randolph in a struggle for better pay and fair treatment. Songs, stories, first-person accounts, and numerous black-and-white photographs accompany the narrative, which is unique in content.

1990 HONORS

GREENFIELD, ELOISE. *Nathaniel Talking.* Illustrated by Jan Spivey Gilchrist. Black Butterfly Children's Books, 1988. Gr. K–3.

Nathaniel is nine years old and his voice is strong in this collection of eighteen poems accompanied by black-and-white illustrations. In the rhythms of blues and rap, this young male voice comes through strong and buoyant. Emotions fill the corners of the poems as Nathaniel reflects and raps about his life. His pride and strength are grounded in his family and his troubles, which he faces with confidence. Nathaniel springs to life, a vibrant, funny, clear-sighted human being.

HAMILTON, VIRGINIA. *The Bells of Christmas.* Illustrated by Lambert Davis. Harcourt Brace Jovanovich, 1989. Gr. K–6.

An elegant tribute to the childlike anticipation of family Christmas observances takes place in 1890 in the Bell family home located on the historic National Road near Springfield, Ohio. Told from the point of view of twelve-year-old Jason Bell, the story offers references to independence, to travel across time and space, and to the historical period. An invigorating sense of this loving African American family's continuity combines with a warm expression of uncommercialized holiday joy.

PATTERSON, LILLIE. *Martin Luther King, Jr., and the Freedom Movement.* Illustrated with photographs. Facts on File, 1989. Gr. 6–8*

Expanding Martin Luther King Jr.'s image from that of a famous African American civil rights leader to that of the human rights leader who won the 1964 Nobel Peace Prize, Patterson's biography offers a reliable transition between juvenile and adult book accounts of the twentieth-century freedom fighter. The biography is illustrated with black-and-white photographs, maps, and freedom songs, and includes an excellent annotated listing of further reading and a brief chronology.

1989 WINNER

MYERS, WALTER DEAN. *Fallen Angels*. Scholastic, 1988. Gr. 9–12.

Using Vietnam for the setting and U.S. teenagers as most of the characters, this landmark novel offers a logical, easy-to-follow story about the often questionable logic of going to war. Seventeen-year-old Richie Perry is the African American protagonist whose medical papers don't catch up with him before he's shipped overseas. The war at home is revealed in letters the soldiers receive from friends and family; however, almost all of the episodes occur in the jungle during tedious hours of waiting, which are occasionally interrupted by minutes of sheer terror and chaos. Although author Myers never moralizes, a highly moral core is evident throughout this mesmerizing novel. Along with Richie Perry's humanity and bravery, the book's depiction of war's brutality will be remembered long after readers finish the book.

1989 HONORS

BERRY, JAMES. *A Thief in the Village and Other Stories.* Orchard, 1987. Gr. 9–12.

The short stories in *A Thief in the Village* present a picturesque glimpse into the day-to-day life of the people in a Jamaican village. The vignettes, which cover a range of emotions from sad to philosophical to humorous, sing with Berry's poetic prose. Becky is among the children that Berry celebrates. She wants a bike so that she can ride with the Wheels-and-Brake Boys. Mum says girls don't do that, but with an all's-well-that-ends-well finish, Becky gets a bike and her widowed Mum gets a boyfriend.

Then there is the pathos in the story of young Gustus, who, during a raging hurricane, nearly loses his life trying to save the banana tree. It was marked as his personal birthright—he had hoped to make money from the sale of the fruit to buy shoes.

In the title story, a sister and brother, Nenna and Man-Man, set up an all-night vigil to catch the thief who has been stealing their coconuts. *A Thief in the Village* is a charming look at the people who live and work in a tropical village that is not always a paradise.

HAMILTON, VIRGINIA. *Anthony Burns: The Defeat and Triumph of a Fugitive Slave.* Knopf, 1988. Gr. 6–12*

Biography and historical fiction are interwoven in a carefully written account of Anthony Burns's 1854 Boston trial based on the controversial federal Fugitive Slave Act of 1793. Documented from primary sources, the biographical portions concerning Burns's imprisonment and trial are interspersed with innovative fictional segments reconstructing his youth as an enslaved child in Virginia. Source notes, a list of persons in the book, excerpts from the Fugitive Slave Act, and the author's comments further increase the value of this unusual illuminating book.

1988 WINNER

TAYLOR, MILDRED D. *The Friendship.* Illustrated by Max Ginsburg. Dial, 1987. Gr. 6–12.

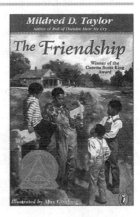

In a powerful short story issued as a single volume, the four Logan children are witnesses to a frightening scene at the general store in Strawberry, Mississippi. When a respected elder in the African American community dares to call the white store owner by his first name, the elder is brutally attacked by a group of white men who are unaware of a decades-long friendship between the two. Mr. Tom Bee refuses to be cowed by the attack, however, and he continues to call out the name of the store owner even after he is lying on the ground, beaten and bleeding. Both literally and figuratively, this deeply moving story shows children a courageous model of active resistance to racism and oppression.

1988 HONORS

DE VEAUX, ALEXIS. *An Enchanted Hair Tale.* Illustrated by Cheryl Hanna. Harper & Row, 1987. Gr. K–2.

Sudan's wonderful hair—"a fan daggle of locks and lions and lagoons"— sets him apart from other kids in his neighborhood, who tease him because he is different. Upset by their cruelty, he storms away and, far from home, stumbles upon a whole family of folks with enchanted hair who help him celebrate his differences. De Veaux's rhythmic text is full of winsome rhyme and alliteration. Her imagery brilliantly conveys the mystery and magic of Sudan's hair. The poem is enhanced and extended by Cheryl Hanna's captivating black-and-white pencil drawings.

LESTER, JULIUS. *The Tales of Uncle Remus: The Adventures of Brer Rabbit.* Introduction by Augusta Baker. Illustrated by Jerry Pinkney. Dial, 1987. Gr. 3–6.

A new Uncle Remus emerges from Lester's creative reshaping of forty-eight Brer Rabbit stories from African American traditions into modified, contemporary southern Black English. Storytelling specialist Augusta Baker's introduction speaks of the importance for contemporary children to hear these tales; Lester's foreword advises telling or reading the tales in one's own language. Occasional black-and-white drawings complement the high-spirited tales, and four watercolors are reproduced in full color on double-page spreads.

1987 WINNER

WALTER, MILDRED PITTS. *Justin and the Best Biscuits in the World.* Lothrop, Lee, & Shepard, 1986. Gr. 3–5.

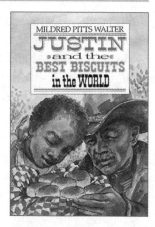

After the death of his father, ten-year-old Justin finds himself living surrounded by women—his mother and his two sisters. There is constant conflict because Justin has very set ideas about what is and is not a man's work. His room is always a mess, washing dishes is not on his list of masculine chores, and if he ever tries to cook anything, the kitchen becomes a disaster. Grandfather Ward comes to the rescue when he takes Justin to his home, a prosperous ranch in Missouri, where Justin learns several lessons about what it takes to be a man. These lessons include how to make a bed, clean the kitchen, and make prize-winning biscuits.

Walter shares a history of the contributions of Black cowboys and, through the grandfather's narration, a lesson in the importance of knowing who you are and where you come from. Justin learns that it is even all right for a man to cry as Grandfather explains his tears and shares a proverb: "The brave hide their fears but share their tears. Tears bathe the soul."

1987 HONORS

BRYAN, ASHLEY. *Lion and the Ostrich Chicks: And Other African Folk Tales.* Atheneum, 1986. Gr. 3–5.

Using his special talent for blending rhythmic word patterns with all the details of a well-told story, Bryan has adapted a diverse collection of African tales that beg to be read aloud. Through his research into the history and culture of several tribes, this author-illustrator found the roots of the stories in many geographical regions and, in his inimitable writing style, retold the tales for young readers. Complete scholar that he is, Bryan has included a bibliography listing his sources for all the stories in the book.

One cannot miss the folktale concept of the triumph of good over evil, whether it is in the title story, in which the lion tries to claim the ostrich chicks as his own, or in a telling of how the born-foolish boy outwits the trickster Ananse.

Bryan extends the text with his own art prints in sharp black-and-white figures or in illustrations using the earth colors of the land in which the tales are set. The Coretta Scott King awards jury enjoyed both the humor and the lessons in *Lion and the Ostrich Chicks*.

HANSEN, JOYCE. *Which Way Freedom?* Walker, 1986. Gr. 6–8.

Obi is a young Union soldier, an escaped slave with haunting memories of being torn from his mother's arms and sold off to a different master. Sustained during his youth by a vague plan to find his mother again he dreamed of an escape with her to Mexico.

Obi learns of the upcoming sale of the farm and enlists the help of old freed slave, Buka, in plotting an escape. On the plantation, Obi, Easter, and young Jason were fast friends. Because of the danger they would face, Obi and Easter must leave young Jason behind as they follow Buka's plans for their escape. Easter and Obi finally part, each seeking a separate way to freedom.

Obi's tense flight ended the moment he joined the advancing Union army, assigned to the Sixth U.S. Artillery of Colored Troops. For the first time, he could call himself by the name he wanted, Obidiah Booker (*Obidiah* meaning "first born" and *Booker* for his faithful counselor and friend, Buka).

1986 WINNER

HAMILTON, VIRGINIA. *The People Could Fly: American Black Folktales.* Illustrated by Leo Dillon and Diane Dillon. Knopf, 1985. Gr. 3–5.

The first comprehensive anthology of African American folklore selected and retold especially for children includes twenty-four exquisitely crafted, individually developed tales. Historical notes accompany each story, and the compilation as a whole is arranged in four categories: trickster tales, tall tales, ghost and devil tales, and stories of liberation and freedom. Hamilton handles information about the Joel Chandler Harris texts with dignity, placing those versions of the traditional tales into a historical context. Her impressive use of Black English from several distinct cultures also distinguishes this excellent collection of folktales.

1986 HONORS

HAMILTON, VIRGINIA. *Junius over Far.* Harper & Row, 1985. Gr. 6–8.

Junius feels a strong connection between himself and his grandfather, who has recently returned to his Caribbean island home. When his grandfather's letters are suddenly filled with obscure references to pirates and kidnapping, Junius convinces his father that they must rush to Grandfather's aid. Shifting points of view give readers insights into the thoughts and feelings of both the teenager and his grandfather, stressing the strength of this intergenerational African American family. Hamilton creates a rich ambience with a lyrical use of language filled with Caribbean cadences and rhythms.

WALTER, MILDRED PITTS. *Trouble's Child.* Lothrop, Lee, & Shepard, 1985. Gr. 6–8.

Set on Blue Island, off the coast of Louisiana, *Trouble's Child* paints a picture of life both simple and complex on the island. The narration shares superstitions, customs, folklore, traditions, and the communal sorrow of an isolated people. Martha, the protagonist, who was born during a storm and is therefore a "trouble child," longs to go to the mainland to study. Her grandmother, Titay, island matriarch and revered midwife, expects Martha to remain on the island and learn from her the secrets of healing herbs and signs. While the folks on the island watch for Martha to bring out her quilting pattern, a signal that she is ready to marry, the stalwart young woman's life is changed. Harold Saunders, an outsider washed ashore during a storm, and Ms. Boudreaux, her teacher, support Martha in her goal to go to school and study science so that she might more effectively help her people. This is an intriguing story, a mix of the old and the new, with a satisfying ending. Walter's use of the island dialect is readable, sensitive, and consistent.

1985 WINNER

MYERS, WALTER DEAN. *Motown and Didi: A Love Story.* Viking, 1984. Gr. 9–12.

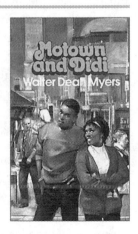

In a story of love, violence, despair, and hope, the unlikely courtship of a homeless young man and an ambitious young woman confronts Harlem's drug culture. Didi's dream of attending college and saving her family from poverty is shattered when she discovers her brother Tony high on dope. Motown lives alone in an abandoned building. His only treasures are books he reads at the suggestion of the Professor—his friend, mentor, and owner of the Spirit of Life bookshop. When Didi reports her brother's dealer to the police, the pusher retaliates, and Motown comes to her rescue. Didi resists the possibility of a romantic attachment, and Motown's experiences with foster care have hardened him against needing anyone.

The leisurely pace of their growing love sets the stage for the work's fast-moving conclusion. When Tony dies of an overdose, Didi begs Motown to kill the pusher who destroyed her brother.

As the Professor and Didi rush toward the impending confrontation between Motown and the dealer, the reality of Harlem surfaces. It is a place where drugs kill while the police take payoffs, where the city administration responds to urban decay by demolishing buildings, leaving empty lots where people dump their garbage. But it is also a place where Motown and Didi find one another.

1985 HONORS

BOYD, CANDY DAWSON. *Circle of Gold.* Apple/Scholastic, 1984. Gr. 4–8.

In the endearing relationship between Mattie and her twin brother Matthew, the two cope with the death of their father and their mother's inability to deal with the loss. Mattie's friend Toni is a reliable and steadfast friend. Two other friends, Angel, whose name is a misnomer, and Charlene, who experiences trouble that results from misplaced loyalties, are less reliable. Through this cast of characters, the reader experiences a theft uncovered, a mother's rehabilitation through therapy, and Mattie's discovery of her own self-worth. The circle of gold is the pin Mattie wins for her mother in an essay contest. The larger circle of gold is the one Mattie discovers when she is convinced of the place she has in her mother's heart.

The spoken and unspoken lessons, and the exploration of human relationships, are highlights of this talented writer's first novel.

HAMILTON, VIRGINIA. *A Little Love.* Philomel, 1984. Gr. 9–12.

Sheema has no memory of her parents: her mother died after Sheema's birth and her father disappeared soon afterward. Her maternal grandparents have raised her with love and great caring, but as she nears graduation from the vocational high school, Sheema feels the need to search for her father. Her knowledge that he's a sign painter who lives somewhere down south is enough to set her on a journey of exploration and discovery, so she and her boyfriend Forrest load up the station wagon and hit the road. An extraordinary story flows from the characterization of an ordinary teenager searching for her identity with the loving support of her friends and family.

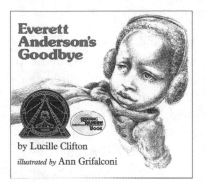

by Lucille Clifton
illustrated by Ann Grifalconi

1984 WINNER

CLIFTON, LUCILLE. *Everett Anderson's Goodbye.* Illustrated by Ann Grifalconi. Holt, Rinehart, & Winston, 1983. Gr. K–2.

In *Everett Anderson's Goodbye*, Lucille Clifton expresses the magnitude of a death in a few gentle words of understanding and compassion. Clifton shares with very young readers the five stages of death, writing with a warmth and a simplicity that transcend any lengthy conversation, serious discussion, or maudlin sentimentality. When his good father dies, Everett begs, promises, questions, and fasts while his mother quietly supports him and lets him know she understands. Ann Grifalconi's expressive black-and-white sketches deepen the mood of this classic, with its memorable closing words:

Whatever happens when people die, love doesn't stop and neither will I.

1984 HONORS

HAMILTON, VIRGINIA. *The Magical Adventures of Pretty Pearl.* Harper & Row, 1983. Gr. 3–5.

When god-child Pretty Pearl announces to her older brothers, John Henry and John de Conqueror, that she would like to try life as a mortal child, they warn her about those humans and their "winning ways" before they send her down from Mount Kenya to try life in the American South during the Reconstruction era. In the midst of a long journey through the South with a cast of characters from African and African American folklore, Pearl comes upon a clandestine self-supporting community of free Blacks whose only link to the outside world is trade with Cherokee and Shawnee Indians. Living among them, Pearl discovers that her brothers were right—she is so drawn to the humans that she must eventually choose between her own immortal power and her newly emerging identity within a struggling mortal community. In a compelling African American odyssey that draws from myth, legend, and history, Hamilton brilliantly explores the relationship between mortal struggle and immortal dreams.

HASKINS, JAMES. *Lena Horne.* Coward-McCann, 1983. Gr. 6–9.

Throughout her successful career as an actress and singer, Lena Horne fought against stereotyping, segregation, and racism by rejecting demeaning roles and by refusing to perform in clubs that treated African Americans unfairly. Her insistence on placing her strong principles over the call of fame and money sometimes cost her work and, in her early years in show business, often made her unpopular among both her peers and her audience. Haskins characterizes the highly visible entertainer as a tough, intelligent, and ambitious woman whose struggles for self-definition began in early childhood and continued throughout her lifetime.

THOMAS, JOYCE CAROL. *Bright Shadow.* Avon, 1983. Gr. 9–12.

Although the writing style is simple, often poetic, the plot of this brief novel is complex. There is a sense of mysticism and the spiritual, with characters beset by strained family relationships, insane cruelty, and death. Abyssinia, called Abby for short, is a sensitive young woman in love with Carl Lee—much to her father's consternation. Many believe that she has the power to "see" things, which gives an aura of suspense to parts of the story. With a sense of relief, the reader finds in the conclusion that after moments of high drama, Abby and Carl Lee will have a life together. *Bright Shadow* is a challenge to the imagination and to the reader's ability to move at times outside the real world.

WALTER, MILDRED PITTS. *Because We Are.* Lothrop, Lee, & Shepard, 1983. Gr. 9–12.

Emma Walsh, an outstanding Black student, is entangled in problems in the all-white school for which she was specially selected. She also finds that she does not fit in when she returns to all-Black Manning High. During her senior year, Emma has to deal with ostracism by her peers, a confrontation with a white teacher who shows only contempt for Manning students, rocky relationships with her divorced parents, and the usual boyfriend-girlfriend complexities.

The intended audience will easily relate to many of the situations in this fast-paced story.

1983 WINNER

HAMILTON, VIRGINIA. *Sweet Whispers, Brother Rush.* Philomel, 1982. Gr. 9–12.

Because her mother's work takes her far from home, fourteen-year-old Tree is often left in charge of the household and caring for her brother, Dabney. She accepts the uncertainty in her life until the day she encounters the ghost of her uncle, Brother Rush, through whom she can go back in time to her early childhood. By reliving key events in the past, Tree begins to ask questions about some of the things left unsaid in her family so that she can begin to understand herself in the broader context of her family's history. This outstanding time-fantasy deals with the complexity of human relationships, the strength of the African American family, and the importance of understanding and acknowledging one's roots.

1983 HONOR

LESTER, JULIUS. *This Strange New Feeling.* Dial, 1982. Gr. 9–12.

This Strange New Feeling is a collection of three well-honed stories, each filled with the creative ingenuity of slaves in an endless quest for freedom. The first tale chronicles the story of Ras and Sally, who help others escape by hiding them in bales of tobacco.

Maria, in "Where the Sun Lives," enjoys a few years of freedom happily married to a freeman who dies suddenly and deeply in debt. Maria is "confiscated" along with other properties that legally can be used to satisfy the lender's claims. Maria approaches the auction block with confidence and dignity. Her spirit will be forever free because she knows "where the sun lives."

"A Christmas Love Story" is a dramatic account of an enslaved couple who make a daring escape to Philadelphia when the wife poses as a young white gentleman traveling north with her dark-skinned servant, William. Tension mounts and danger lurks at every stop along the four-day journey to freedom. Ellen and William Craft flee to England to escape the vengeance that was an integral part of President William Fillmore's Fugitive Slave Bill.

Lester includes research sources for each of the historically based events.

1982 WINNER

TAYLOR, MILDRED D. *Let the Circle Be Unbroken.*
Dial, 1981. Gr. 9–12.

Continuing the story begun in *Song of the Trees*
(1975) and *Roll of Thunder, Hear My Cry* (1976),
Mildred D. Taylor creates a sequel of epic pro-
portions as the Logans face the impact of a racist government policy that threatens their farm.
They must draw on the mutual support and
strength of the African American community
to pull through in a time of crisis. As in previ-
ous volumes, protagonist Cassie's gradual maturation is reflected by her
ever-enlarging world and ever-increasing understanding of the complexities of adulthood.

1982 HONORS

CHILDRESS, ALICE. *Rainbow Jordan.* Coward, McCann, & Geoghegan, 1981.
Gr. 6–12.

Women of four generations are portrayed as fourteen-year-old Rainbow
attempts to find hope and promise in her life. Her mother was a child herself when she became a parent and is of little help to Rainbow. The mother's
youth, inexperience, and lack of education have led to an unstable relationship between mother and child. Instead, Rainbow's involvement with other
women of differing social and economic classes helps her find out who she is
with respect to demands from a foster parent, a social worker, a boyfriend,
and others. Characterizations are splendid, and authentic language is used
skillfully.

HUNTER, KRISTIN. *Lou in the Limelight.* Scribner, 1981. Gr. 9–12.

Hunter's scathing chronicle of the music business is a sequel to her pioneering *Soul Brothers and Sister Lou.* The song "Lament for Jethro," about a friend
killed in a police raid on Lou's brother's printing shop, has become a hit and
Lou and the group have come to New York under the stewardship of their
manager, Marty Ross. Marty, determined to break up the solidarity of the

group by promoting Lou at the expense of the boys, keeps them in virtual servitude as they live in debt while he manipulates their accounts.

In Las Vegas, a member of the group acquires a line of credit that encourages his gambling, all the young performers become drug abusers, and Lou comes to realize that there is a price for everything. Marty steals their copyrights, forces the group to work as an opening act for a white singer, and, finally, a promised movie deal brings the group to a pornographic film studio.

In the midst of their troubles, the group derives strength from Jethro's mother, Aunt Jerutha, who comes to care for them, and from Ben Carroll, a U.S. attorney determined to expose whites in the music business who are taking advantage of Black youth. Their harrowing experiences do not break the young singers as their journey provides an opportunity for self-exploration.

MEBANE, MARY E. *Mary: An Autobiography.* Viking, 1981. Gr. 9–12*

This painfully honest story of growing up in the rural South in the 1930s and 1940s chronicles the struggles of a determined and talented young woman who always felt like an outsider, even within her own family. Young Mary's distinctive personal story is set against the detailed backdrop of the ordinary and familiar day-to-day life of an African American community in rural North Carolina.

1981 WINNER

POITIER, SIDNEY. *This Life.* Knopf, 1980. Gr. 9–12*

This Life is a candid, outspoken autobiography of the noted actor and film star Sidney Poitier. Previous to his birth, Poitier's parents had left Cat Island in the Bahamas to try to make a better living.

Poitier faced many challenges before gaining public notice. He attempts to earn a living by parking cars. Many an accident was the result. When a restaurant in the Deep South refused them service, Poitier and his U.S. Army comrades participated in the total destruction of the place. He speaks of voice and speech training aimed at getting rid of his island accent. Poitier describes the belabored steps from bit-part actor to Academy Award winner.

The book includes his activities offstage and off-screen, his marriages, his friendship and conflict with Harry Belafonte, and his work with the cause espoused by Martin Luther King Jr. *This Life* is a thoughtful yet well-paced study of one man's view of himself and the world around him.

1981 HONOR

DE VEAUX, ALEXIS. *Don't Explain: A Song of Billie Holiday.* Harper & Row, 1980. Gr. 9–12*

Alexis De Veaux's respect and admiration for the singer Billie Holiday reaches out from every page of this factual, poetically written biography. The author does not dismiss the erring ways of which the singer has been accused. Nor does she overlook the high-handed manner in which Holiday was treated by the law. The story tells of some happy days and some days of hope when Holiday's family migrated to Harlem, reaching for the "good life" in the North. As a fledgling blues singer, Holiday was likened to the late Bessie Smith, and the comparison didn't stop there because Holiday also felt the sting of racism that allegedly led to Bessie Smith's death. De Veaux's descriptions of Holiday's bout with drugs and her mercurial career, which ended with the singer strapped to a bed in a prison hospital, are written with a haunting beauty that ensures that readers will remember the Billie Holiday story with a combination of anger for what might questionably be called justice and tears for talent too soon lost.

1980 WINNER

MYERS, WALTER DEAN. *The Young Landlords.* Viking, 1979. Gr. 6–8.

When a group of Harlem teenagers complain to the landlord about the condition of a tenement on their block, he sells it to them for one dollar so that they themselves can take responsibility for its repair and upkeep. With a great deal of warmth and humor, Myers offers young readers an appealing story about a group of ordinary kids who find out firsthand that, although there are no easy solutions to tough problems, the first step toward making the world a better place to live is to work together.

1980 HONORS

GORDY, BERRY, SR. *Movin' Up: Pop Gordy Tells His Story.* Introduction by Alex Haley. Harper & Row, 1979. Gr. 8–12*

The father of the founder of Motown Records tells his own life story, beginning with his childhood in Georgia, when his father always took him along on business transactions because he recognized the boy's shrewd mind for figures. Gordy's business skills sharpened as he grew older and continued working on the family farm. When the sale of timber stumps from his land netted him $2,600, Gordy wisely decided to travel north to Detroit to cash the check rather than to raise the suspicions of unscrupulous white neighbors. He soon sent for the rest of his family to join him, and within a few months he had saved enough money to open a grocery store. All eight of his children worked in the store, and each one grew to be successful. However, it was his seventh son, Berry Gordy Jr., who seemed to follow most closely in his father's footsteps when it came to business. A fascinating picture of a gentle, and remarkably humble, overachiever emerges from this extraordinary autobiography that reads like an oral history.

GREENFIELD, ELOISE, AND LESSIE JONES LITTLE. *Childtimes: A Three-Generation Memoir.* Harper & Row, 1979. Gr. 4–8*

Three women—storytellers and writers, mothers and daughters—each speak in their own distinct voices. Photographs from the family album combine with each woman's remembrances of her "childtimes" to produce an unforgettable personal glimpse into history.

Pattie Frances Ridley Jones, born December 15, 1884, was close to the slave days and remembers her mother, who worked as an unpaid maid for the family that had owned Pattie's grandmother before emancipation. Lessie Blanche Jones Little, born October 1, 1906, writes of her girlhood days and adolescence. Eloise Glynn Little Greenfield, born May 17, 1929, writes of her North Carolina birthplace.

Each voice speaks of home, family, chores, social events, and courtship. In a direct style, deceptively simple, each woman tells of the fears and hopes, poverty and hunger, love and pride, laughter and music during her growing-up years. This unique and vibrant compilation has an effect that is poignant and moving. The patterns of the telling link one child to the next and all three children to the reader. Few books have brought the everyday life of history to readers so vividly and effectively.

HASKINS, JAMES. *Andrew Young: Young Man with a Mission.* Illustrated with photographs. Lothrop, Lee, & Shepard, 1979. Gr. 9–12*

The son of an affluent dentist in New Orleans, Andrew Young was a precocious child who started kindergarten at age three and graduated from Howard University when he was just nineteen. He became an activist in the Civil Rights Movement as a young minister in Thomasville, Georgia, and his talents as a diplomat and organizer soon thrust him into a leadership role within the Southern Christian Leadership Conference). In 1972, he became the first African American congressman elected from the South since the Reconstruction era, and in 1976 he was appointed by President Jimmy Carter as the U.S. ambassador to the United Nations. In the arena of international politics, Ambassador Young became known for his directness and for his unwavering stand for human rights, a stance that was often critical of the U.S. power structure. This straightforward biography does not shy away from the controversy that surrounded Andrew Young in his public life.

HASKINS, JAMES. *James Van DerZee: The Picture Takin' Man.* Illustrated with Van DerZee photographs. Dodd, Mead, 1979. Gr. 6–9*

The work of James Van DerZee was unrecognized and virtually unknown in the art world until his photographs of Harlem in the 1920s and 1930s were featured in a 1968 exhibition at the Metropolitan Museum of Art entitled "Harlem on My Mind." At the time, the photographer was eighty-three years old. Because James Van DerZee's life spanned the twentieth century, because he had been able to document in photographs only a small part of what his trained eye had seen over the years, and because very little had been written about him for either adults or children, Haskins was determined to get the full story down in print by conducting interviews and corresponding with the man himself. This engaging account, based on those interviews, creates a portrait with words of the intelligent, hardworking, and dignified man who became known for his portraits of African Americans—men, women, and children of Harlem who shared the traits of the man behind the camera.

SOUTHERLAND, ELLEASE. *Let the Lion Eat Straw.* Scribner, 1979. Gr. 9–12.

Abeba Williams spent her early years in the nurturing care of Mamma Habbleshaw in rural North Carolina. Abeba's tranquil life was changed when her natural mother took her to New York. Abeba is a strong, sensitive character who grows from childhood to womanhood under a variety of circumstances. She survives her mother's sometimes volatile temper, the incestuous advances of an uncle, and a marriage to a man who she later learns has a history of insanity. After raising a very large family and using her musical talent as a sustaining force, Abeba dies in peace, a well-respected woman in the community. *Let the Lion Eat Straw* is a moving story, written in rhythmic, poetic prose. It is the story of a truly genteel woman.

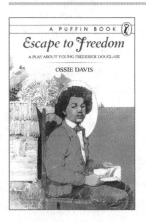

1979 WINNER

DAVIS, OSSIE. *Escape to Freedom: A Play about Young Frederick Douglass.* Viking, 1978. Gr. 6–8.

Ossie Davis, playwright and actor, lends his artistic talent to the writing of a play that affords young readers a chance to reenact scenes from the life of the abolitionist Frederick Douglass. The scenes are dramatic and forthright, withholding none of the vindictiveness of cruel slave masters, as if to forcefully demonstrate the reasons for Douglass's determination to escape to freedom. The play tells of Douglass's accomplishments as a lecturer, a newspaper editor, and a fighter for women's rights at a time when such things were basically unheard of. Douglass's fighting spirit is summed up in a speech made after he whipped his master in a "fair fight":

I'm free . . . I know I'm still in bondage but I got a feeling—the most important feeling in the world—I'm free.

Freedom songs are interspersed among the scenes, and there are directions for staging. However, strict copyright limitations seem to have been placed on the use of the script for "other than personal reading." But even in that context, this powerful minidrama is well worth reading and sharing.

1979 HONORS

FENNER, CAROL. *The Skates of Uncle Richard.* Illustrated by Ati Forberg. Random House, 1978. Gr. K–2.

The star skating champion who once fueled the dreams of nine-year-old Marsha disappears when the ice skates she'd hoped for at Christmas turn out to be ugly, old-fashioned hockey skates that once belonged to her uncle. But the dream skater gradually returns after Marsha gets an impromptu skating lesson and a demonstration of some fancy footwork on the ice from the former owner of the skates. This is an easy-to-read transition to books divided into chapters—and a story that shows how hard work and determination are essential to making dreams come true.

HAMILTON, VIRGINIA. *Justice and Her Brothers.* Greenwillow, 1978. Gr. 3–5.

At first, eleven-year-old Justice blames the pervasive sense of eeriness enveloping her home on the fact that it's the first summer she and her older brothers have been left on their own during the day while their dad is at work and their mom is enrolled in college classes. But gradually, she, her brothers, and their young neighbor, Dorian, begin to realize that the telepathic powers they all possess are greatly heightened when they work together as a unit. To their great surprise, they also realize that Justice is genetically predestined for greatness as their leader, a fact that doesn't sit well with her older brother Thomas. The compelling, original science fiction story is rooted in the reality of small-town family life, sibling rivalry, and a young girl's transformation from a fretting, uncertain child into a confident young woman ready to face whatever challenges the future may hold.

PATTERSON, LILLIE. *Benjamin Banneker: Genius of Early America.* Illustrated by David Scott Brown. Abingdon, 1978. Gr. 3–5*

Born on his family's tobacco farm in Maryland on November 9, 1731, Benjamin Banneker's grandmother, Molly Walsh, an English indentured servant, taught him to read. His grandfather, the son of a tribal king in Senegal, and his father, a freed slave from Guinea, taught him to observe the world of plants and animals around him. In a school opened by a Quaker neighbor, Banneker learned literature, history, and mathematics.

Lillie Patterson details the impact Banneker's lifelong fascination with numbers and technology had on his neighbors and ultimately his country.

He built the first clock made entirely from parts manufactured in the colonies; he calculated accurate almanacs to guide farmers, fishermen, and sailors; and, at Thomas Jefferson's suggestion, he was appointed by George Washington to help survey the new nation's capital. When Pierre L'Enfant walked out on the project and returned to France with his plans, it was Banneker's expertise and continued involvement that made possible the realization of those plans in the beautiful design of Washington, D.C.

Patterson combines facts with fictionalized conversations and distinguishes between fact and myth, providing enough information to dramatize these important historical moments.

PETERSON, JEANNE WHITEHOUSE. *I Have a Sister, My Sister Is Deaf.* Harper & Row, 1977. Gr. K–2.

In prose that has the rhythm of poetry, Jeanne Whitehouse Peterson has written a story that will speak to all who work with those who cannot hear. As a loving and patient sister, she tells the reader how a deaf person understands certain things, such as the barking of a dog contrasted with the purring of a cat sitting in the person's lap. She makes note of things that bring fright to a hearing child but that do not bother the deaf child—such as a clap of thunder on a stormy night or the banging of a shutter when the wind is high. She talks of the companionship that is shared as the sisters walk through the woods: "I am the one who listens for small sounds. She is the one who watches for quick movements in the grass." The illustrations in this gentle explanatory book show a multiethnic group of children sharing in the experience of the one who has a sister who is deaf.

1978 WINNER

GREENFIELD, ELOISE. *Africa Dream.* *Illustrated by Carole Byard.* John Day, 1977. Gr. K–2.

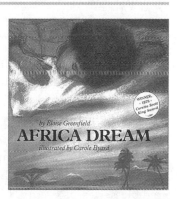

At first glance, Byard's pencil sketches seem airy and dreamlike, but a closer look reveals subtle details that give a sense of reality to the far-off African homeland to which a young child's imagination takes her. There is an impressive amount of historical information provided through the words and images. The illustrations of noble rulers of long ago, classic architecture, and graceful people make *Africa Dream* a book of visible pride and dignity.

1978 HONORS

FAULKNER, WILLIAM J. *The Days When the Animals Talked: Black American Folktales and How They Came to Be.* Illustrated by Troy Howell. Follett, 1977. Gr. 3–6.

Looking back on his childhood, the African American folklorist William J. Faulkner shares stories both real and imagined. Many of the tales derive from stories he heard from a former slave, Simon Brown, who came as a freed man to work for the Faulkner family. In part 1, the reader encounters the hardships of slavery, the frustrating powerlessness of the men and women enslaved by masters who used them as they pleased—in terms of work, sex, and aggression. Faulkner tells these stories without rancor but with a depth of feeling that stirs deep emotions.

In part 2, Faulkner tells animal stories, sharing vital information about the symbolic importance of Brer Rabbit and his companions. In an introduction to this section Faulkner states:

"Signs of unrest, dissatisfaction and even outright protest are easy to detect in some of the longer dramatic tales. As the animals behaved in the stories so the slaves were motivated to behave in their struggle to survive. Although weaponless and defenseless, the slaves, like the small animals, could at times get the better of their powerful adversaries through cunning, careful planning and occasionally social action."

GLASS, FRANKCINA. *Marvin and Tige.* St. Martin's, 1977. Gr. 6–10.

At age eleven, Tige is an illiterate African American street urchin on his own after the sudden death of his mother. He survives by his wit and his ability to steal and to find adequate shelter. Finally, this continuous fight for survival gets the best of him and he plans suicide. At that moment, in steps Marvin, a down-and-out, once-upon-a-time successful businessman. This unlikely interracial combination teams up and begins to make life livable—two lonely people who have found solace in each other. In a hardly credible series of events, Marvin finds Tige's father, who had abandoned

Tige's mother before the child's birth. Marvin convinces Richard Davis that he must give his son a rightful place in his family. The bittersweet ending sees Tige established in his new home but with the ties to his friend Marvin still intact. This is a warm story with touches of humor, discussions about religious beliefs, and ideas about death and the value of education. It is the story of two people who care about each other with a relationship unencumbered by racial differences.

GREENFIELD, ELOISE. *Mary McLeod Bethune.* Crowell, 1977. Gr. K–4*

This sympathetic portrayal of one of the great heroines in American history is simply told but never simplistic. Greenfield skillfully weaves into the personal history of Mary McLeod Bethune aspects of post–Civil War life in America and the trauma of segregation. This straightforward telling of Bethune's unflagging devotion to making the lives of Black people better through education includes a brief introduction to some of the noted personalities with whom she worked to attain her goal—money for her educational projects. Particularly interesting is the discussion of her working relationship and warm friendship with Eleanor Roosevelt. Bethune's endless struggles to make her dreams come true are as impressive as her ability to bring African Americans together to solve problems long neglected by the establishment.

HASKINS, JAMES. *Barbara Jordan.* Illustrated with photographs. Dial, 1977. Gr. 6–10*

Barbara Jordan, a former congresswoman from Texas, first came to national attention as a member of the House Judiciary Committee during the Watergate hearings in 1974. Her strongly held opinions won her friends and enemies in political circles. James Haskins captures the complexity of Barbara Jordan and her times through the eyes of her supporters and her critics. Although this biography focuses on Jordan's life as a leading political figure in Washington, D.C., Haskins provides additional information that more fully describes her dynamic personality.

Barbara Jordan's eloquent speaking ability and decisive critical thinking skills were nurtured from early childhood by her maternal grandfather. She continued developing these skills on the debating team at Texas Southern University.

Jordan's political career was marked with defeat the first few times she sought office: in 1962, when she ran for the Texas House of Representatives, and again in 1964. Jordan won her seat in the Texas House of Representatives in 1965, the first African American in the Texas House since 1883. Haskins describes Jordan's career as a member of the U.S. House of Representatives (taking office in January 1973), her appointment to the powerful Judiciary Committee, and her influential discourse during the Watergate hearings.

PATTERSON, LILLIE. *Coretta Scott King.* Garrard, 1977. Gr. 3–5*

This biography begins with the talented Coretta Scott's dilemma of choosing between a musical career and the man she loves. She assumes the role of wife and mother during the years of the organized, nonviolent civil rights protests in the South. Beginning with the Montgomery bus boycott in 1955, when the threat of violence was nearly constant, Patterson recognizes the strength and stability Coretta Scott King brought to her family and their friends and acquaintances. The emphasis is on her self-sacrifice and dedication to family. The only time she raises her voice, writes Patterson, is after a sleepless night during which she received forty hate calls. The book imparts well the nonviolent attitude the Kings had to practice in their personal and private lives to stay focused on the larger goal of civil rights.

STEWART, RUTH ANN. *Portia: The Life of Portia Washington Pittman, the Daughter of Booker T. Washington.* Doubleday, 1977. Gr. 6–9*

Portia Washington Pittman lived a riches-to-almost rags life with admirable dignity. Awareness of the stature and importance of her renowned father, Booker T. Washington, permeated her childhood. Notably, despite Booker T. Washington's outspoken support of segregation, he sent his only daughter to northern schools and colleges where she was the only Black allowed to enroll. As a young woman, Portia traveled abroad to study piano under a German master musician.

The biography recalls Portia Washington's meeting with her father's adversary, W. E. B. Du Bois; her dining with presidents; her studying under George Washington Carver; her marriage to architect Sidney Pittman; and the birth and death of her three children. The writer describes Portia Pittman's slow decline into poverty following her dismissal from the faculty of

Tuskegee Institute, her living in squalor in Washington, D.C.; and finally her dying at age ninety in peace and dignity in a home provided for her by members of the Washington, D.C., Tuskegee Alumni Association. Black-and-white photographs give an added dimension to this well-documented biography.

1977 WINNER

HASKINS, JAMES. *The Story of Stevie Wonder.* Illustrated with photographs. Lothrop, Lee, & Shepard, 1976. Gr. 6–10*

A powerful story of remarkable achievement emerges from this well-written biography of a popular singer, songwriter, and musician. Blind from birth, Steveland Morris was always encouraged by his family to explore and develop his other senses, especially his senses of touch and hearing. While he was still a toddler, his mother bought him a set of cardboard drums and a toy harmonica. Stevie's musical abilities became so well known around his community that friends and neighbors bought him a real drum set, a real harmonica, and, when he was seven years old, a secondhand piano. By the time he came to the attention of Motown Records a few years later, he was already an accomplished musician, and Motown called him "Little Stevie Wonder, the twelve-year-old genius." Haskins tells Stevie Wonder's story by tracing his personal as well as his musical accomplishments.

1977 HONORS

BLAKE, CLARENCE N., AND DONALD F. MARTIN. *Quiz Book on Black America.* Houghton Mifflin, 1976. Gr. 6 9*

Based on scholarly research, the *Quiz Book on Black America* contains probing questions about the achievements and contributions of Black Americans in every aspect of American life. The format of the book allows the user to concentrate on an area of special interest or to browse through questions in various subject areas: education, business, sports, the arts, and social action. The book covers a broad time line, with quizzes ranging from events in the mid-nineteenth century to the time of the book's publication, fulfilling its stated purpose to "make the acquisition of knowledge a pleasurable experience."

CLIFTON, LUCILLE. *Everett Anderson's Friend.* Illustrated by Ann Grifalconi. Holt, Rinehart, & Winston, 1976. Gr. K–3.

In a series of books, the voice of Everett Anderson has spoken to young readers through the words of a poet who understands childhood concerns. In "real boy" fashion, Everett Anderson takes a dislike to his neighbor, Maria. How could he like a girl who can beat him in racing and play ball better than he can! But when Everett Anderson loses his key and goes into Maria's apartment until his mother comes home, everything changes. Everett Anderson finds friendship in Apartment 3A—and even learns something about food from the Hispanic culture. With bouncy verse and quick poetic sketches, Clifton, a gifted storyteller, provides young readers not only with a joyful verse but also, more important, with a slice-of-life experience worthy of being remembered. Ann Grifalconi's illustrations capture the warmth of the author's text.

TAYLOR, MILDRED D. *Roll of Thunder, Hear My Cry.* Dial, 1976. Gr. 6–12.

Set in rural Mississippi during the Depression, this novel chronicles the lives of a strong African American family struggling to hold on to their land as seen through the eyes of their young daughter, Cassie. Despite hard times, economically and socially, the extended Logan family fills its household with love, security, and dignity, creating and maintaining an environment from which all family members draw the strength they need to face the rigors of everyday life in the segregated South.

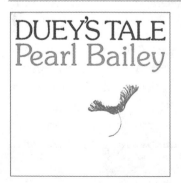

DUEY'S TALE
Pearl Bailey

1976 WINNER

BAILEY, PEARL. *Duey's Tale.* Harcourt Brace Jovanovich, 1975. Gr. 4–6.

The poetic prose of *Duey's Tale* reflects the music and life experiences of Pearl Bailey. In a tale set in a philosophical mood, Duey, a seedling from a maple tree, makes observations about life and about finding out who one really is and learns a great lesson about friendship. As a seedling, Duey finds himself rudely stripped from his mother roots by a strong gust of wind. While bemoaning his loss of security, he finds adventure with a friendly log and a glass bottle. The three companions share pleasant moments together until the time comes for each to take its destined special place in the scheme of things—places that are marked by change. A saddened but wiser and mature Duey, now a sturdy maple tree, concludes that being different is not so bad, but what really matters is that everyone "needs a little attention, and that's why people have family and friends."

1976 HONORS

GRAHAM, SHIRLEY. *Julius K. Nyerere: Teacher of Africa.* Messner, 1975. Gr. 6–9*

A biography that was welcomed at the time of its publication, this book supports the view of President Nyerere as a dedicated, modest leader-teacher who worked to liberate Tanganyika and then Zanzibar and to join the two as the new country of Tanzania. Written for young people, the book lucidly explains Nyerere's political philosophy, which views society as an extended family and which incorporates both tradition and tribal pride into its political system. Graham's view of Nyerere is positive. The repressive policies and interparty disputes at work in Tanzania at the time are discussed, although interpreted to fit with the generally positive view of Nyerere. The author successfully employs both fictional dialogue and excerpts from Nyerere's writings.

GREENFIELD, ELOISE. *Paul Robeson.* Illustrated by George Ford. Crowell, 1975. Gr. 3–6*

Greenfield offers the story of Paul Robeson to young readers in easily accessible language. She smoothly compresses Robeson's personal story with his accomplishments as athlete, stage actor, and political activist. His developing political commitment and the repressive reaction against it are presented in honest, unbiased terms. The timbre, style, and impact of Robeson's musical performances are clearly conveyed. In addition, the effort and determination it took for young Robeson to succeed as an athlete are expressed in terms that children can easily understand and relate to. This impressive man's unswerving dedication to pursuing justice and opposing oppression for Black and poor people is offered with obvious respect, in clear and simple terms.

MYERS, WALTER DEAN. *Fast Sam, Cool Clyde, and Stuff.* Viking, 1975. Gr. 6–12.

When Stuff was twelve and one-half years old, his family moved to 116th Street in Harlem. Six years later, he recounts his extraordinary first year with the friends he found there.

Myers is frank about the problems faced on 116th Street. The group's sense of community helps them face these challenges, as does Stuff's ability to find absurdity in adversity.

Myers's wit, conveyed in his characters' language, expresses the humorous aspects of hurtful situations. When Binky's ear is bitten off during a fight, Clyde suggests a hospital visit to have it reattached. The doctor sees the frantic young people as threatening hoodlums and alerts the authorities, who ask them to roll up their sleeves and puts them in jail as if they were junkies.

By the time Stuff comes to record his memories, the neighborhood has altered, the friends have dispersed. The book, then, is about a brief moment in Stuff's life, the world in which he lived, the community that helped him confront that world, and the universal need to find such a community in our own lives.

TAYLOR, MILDRED D. *Song of the Trees.* Dial, 1975. Gr. 3–5.

Eight-year-old Cassie Logan loves the majestic old trees on her family's property almost as much as her daddy does. When two powerful white men scheme to cut down the trees for lumber, Mr. Logan comes up with a scheme of his own to foil the trespassers. Taylor's first published children's book shows the emergence of traits that would become the author's trademark in subsequent work: excellent characterizations, a strong sense of place, and the ability to weave a great story by drawing together threads of social history, the rural South, and African American family life.

1975 WINNER

ROBINSON, DOROTHY. *The Legend of Africania.* Illustrated by Herbert Temple. Johnson Publishing, 1974. Gr. K–3.

The Legend of Africania is a multilevel tale. Africania is a beautiful maiden living in the harmony of her African homeland and beloved by Prince Uhuru. On a fateful day, Africania is bewitched by the evil, pale-skinned Takata. She is taken to another land and imprisoned until she decides to become pale like Takata, to take on the pale-faced spirit's ways. Only when she learns that this imitation is the real prison does she become free and united with her lover, Prince Uhuru. On one level, this story is written with the flavor of the traditional folktale. The Coretta Scott King awards jury "read into it a much more significant story—almost an allegory. It is seen as a story of slavery, of resistance to a master's domination, and as a lesson in remembering to always take pride in one's blackness."

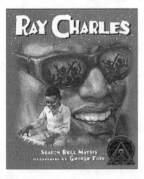

1974 WINNER

MATHIS, SHARON BELL. *Ray Charles.* Illustrated by George Ford. Crowell, 1973. Gr. K–3*

This simplified biography gives young readers a glimpse into the life of a talented musician who, though blind, refused to see himself as disabled. The author highlights episodes from the childhood accident that caused the blindness to Ray Charles's special education and, finally, his triumph as a performer of international fame. In this inspirational portrayal, Ray Charles is seen not as handicapped but as *handicapable.*

1974 HONORS

CHILDRESS, ALICE. *A Hero Ain't Nothin' but a Sandwich.* Coward, McCann, & Geoghegan, 1973. Gr. 6–12.

Benjie Johnson is thirteen and "ain't a chile no more." He is a junkie, and his habit is destroying his life and ripping apart his family. Benjie's story unfolds from the perspective of his family, friends, and teachers.

Benjie's father has left, and his mother is ready to marry Butler Craig, who lives with the mother and son. When Benjie flees across the roof of his building, however, Butler saves the boy from a near fall down an airshaft. His tenuous hold on Benjie and the precipitous drop down the shaft become metaphors for their relationship.

Benjie promises to report regularly to a detoxification program, and Butler will support him by meeting him there. But as the book ends, Butler is getting cold waiting for Benjie to arrive, not sure if Benjie can see him where he is standing, not sure if Benjie is late or not coming.

"The wind is blowing colder now, but if I go in—he might get this far, then lose courage. Come on, Benjie, I believe in you. . . . It's nation time. . . . I'm waiting for you. . . ."

CLIFTON, LUCILLE. *Don't You Remember?* Illustrated by Evaline Ness. Dutton, 1973. Gr. K–2.

A familiar theme is treated with warm family love in this gentle "lap" story. Desire Mary Tate is sure that her family can never remember anything because her father postpones taking her to the plant where he works as an engineer, her mother doesn't bring home the black cake with the pink letters, and not one of her big brothers will give her the promised taste of coffee. Repeating her favorite phrase of total exasperation, "Dag, double dag," Tate retreats to her room and eventually to bed. What a surprise when the next morning—after sleeping late—Tate is awakened to find that not only will she go to the plant, but because it is her birthday she also will have the black cake with pink letters *and* coffee. In simple language that is not condescending, Clifton captures a young child's concerns. The book invites adults to read it aloud to the many little ones who feel left out and who fear that grown-ups do not remember those things that are terribly important in young lives.

CRANE, LOUISE. *Ms. Africa: Profiles of Modern African Women.* Lippincott, 1973. Gr. 6–9*

This collection of biographies pays tribute to women from various geographical regions of Africa who have made significant achievements in widely diverse fields. Included is the intriguing story of a woman engineer, with one of the longest names imaginable—a combination of her father's name, her husband's name, and her feminine name—who was in charge of managing the water supply for all residents in Madagascar. Her knowledge and ability finally gained the respect of the men she supervised. Efua Sutherland, a writer and a teacher from Ghana, was a catalyst for having authentic African stories published in many languages. Sutherland became interested in writing for children when she observed the dearth of Ghanian literature written for young audiences. As a part of this interest, she studied folklore and involved groups in the dramatization of stories based on the trickster Ananse.

Lawyers, models, political activists, civil servants, and members of the medical profession are all a part of this book about women of color who achieved despite racial and political odds against them.

HUNTER, KRISTIN. *Guests in the Promised Land.* Scribner, 1973. Gr. 9–12.

Hunter speaks in the voices of young men and women in the process of defining themselves and their relationship with an often-hostile society.

In "Hero's Return," Jody encounters his big brother Junior, home after eighteen months "in the house" for armed robbery. Jody expects to find a hero, but instead he meets a brother determined to impress upon him that jail is not the romanticized retreat of street-corner fantasies.

In the tragicomedy of "BeeGee's Ghost," Freddy must arrange for a proper funeral for his dog because the pet cemetery will not accept "colored dogs." Having buried BeeGee in the backyard, Freddy wryly notes, "I'll never stop wondering how some folks can hate other folks so much they'd take it out on a little dog."

In the title story, "Guests in the Promised Land," the young people are welcomed to play on the Cedarbrook Country Club Grounds. It was not Robert's fault that the trip arranged by white businessmen did not work out. The sign on the door of the elegant dining room pointedly noted, "Guests not allowed without members."

" . . . It ain't no Promised Land at all if some people are always guests and others are always members."

NAGENDA, JOHN. *Mukasa.* Illustrated by Charles Lilly. Macmillan, 1973. Gr. 3–5*

In this book, based on the author's life, Nagenda's autobiography tells of a young boy in Africa who realizes the joy and importance of an education. Mukasa was born to his parents late in their lives and became a protected "treasure" to his mother, much to his father's chagrin. When Mukasa's father would not help raise the money to send the boy to school, the boy's creative mother found a way to do it. Through Mukasa's eyes, one learns something of the educational system in his village at the time of the story and of the ingenuity of the teacher who, lacking a great supply of commercial teaching materials, creatively provided students with effective homemade learning tools. In this simple setting, one gains a little insight into the activities and pranks that are a part of just about every schoolchild's experience. One might accept as a high point of the book the closing incident when upon Mukasa's return home after graduation, his father asks Mukasa to teach him how to read. It is then that Mukasa decides, "Perhaps I won't be a doctor after all. Now I think I'll be a teacher."

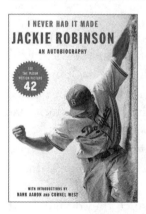

1973 WINNER

DUCKETT, ALFRED. *I Never Had It Made: The Autobiography of Jackie Robinson.* Putnam, 1972. Gr. 6–10*

With candor, Jackie Robinson describes the difficulties of being the first Black to play in major league baseball—racially motivated problems, threats of physical violence from ballplayers on his and on opposing teams, and cruel criticism from several sportswriters. Talent was not enough in a sport dominated by white players and white administrators.

Robinson does not try to gloss over personal problems that he and wife Rachel faced while trying to raise their children in the segregated South and in predominantly white areas in the North. The children seemingly suffered identity problems—and for at least one, with tragic results.

In writing of his days after baseball, Robinson discusses the trials and tribulations of working in a management position for Chock full o' Nuts. He also relates his attempts to work with the NAACP until what he calls "The Old Guard" forced his resignation. In conclusion, this public hero explains the book's title, attesting that despite his success and triumphs, as a Black man in a white world, he "never had it made."

1972 WINNER

FAX, ELTON. *17 Black Artists*. Dodd, Mead, 1971. Gr. 6–10*

Using as a catalyst a slogan he read in Africa, "Sweet Are the Uses of Adversity," Elton Fax researched the lives of seventeen African American artists who succeeded against the odds. Not only do the biographical sketches paint pictures of the artists as people, but each one also provides a picture of the social climate in which the individual lived and worked.

Race chauvinism veered white artists away from such a course, and the Black artist, eager for commission, dared not risk offending his white clientele.

Fax pays tribute to an early-twentieth-century artist, James Herring, who, despite skeptics, established an art department at Howard University in 1921. Included is a chapter on Romare Bearden, who, before his death in 1988, left a legacy of illustrations for young people in *A Visit to the Country* (Harper & Row, 1989). Jacob Lawrence and Faith Ringgold are also included in this compendium.

The book is a valuable volume in the annals of African American history and, even more important, a valuable study of the life and work of serious artists who happen to be Black.

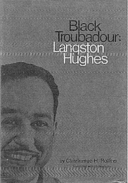

1971 WINNER

ROLLINS, CHARLEMAE. *Black Troubadour: Langston Hughes*. Rand McNally, 1970. Gr. 6–12*

Langston Hughes's poetry and prose capture the rhythms of the blues and the richness of African American speech. Charlemae Rollins met Hughes when she was the children's librarian at the George

C. Hall branch of the Chicago Public Library. Hughes was writing and discussing poetry with members of the Illinois Writers Project.

Rollins writes of the loving influence of Hughes's maternal grandmother, contrasting this life with the troubled visits with his father who had settled in Mexico. Rollins includes Hughes's experiences in New York's Harlem, his disappointment in the large and impersonal classes at New York University, and the segregation at Columbia University.

Eventually, Hughes graduated from Lincoln University in Pennsylvania while continuing to call his beloved Harlem home. His relationship with Mary McLeod Bethune was the impetus for poetry tours of the South and where—through his poetry-reading concerts—he was able to support himself and concentrate on his writing.

Hughes's seemingly simple language becomes a profound comment on the America he found in his travels:

> Where is the Jim Crow section
> On this merry-go-round,
> Mister, cause I want to ride?

Rollins cites the large number of now familiar images that have entered the vernacular from his creative pen. She describes the successes and discouragements of his life, his ultimate hope, and his death in 1967.

1971 HONORS

ANGELOU, MAYA. *I Know Why the Caged Bird Sings.* Random House, 1969. Gr. 8–12*

In this biography, Maya Angelou explores the innermost depth of her personal self. With a masterful use of poetic prose, she invokes moments of laughter, anger, tears, and shouts of victory for justice triumphant. As a youngster in Stamps, Arkansas, she experiences the sting of racial prejudice and of family betrayal but also the support of her wise and compassionate brother Bailey. She pays tribute to her uncle Willie, from whom she learned her multiplication tables as well as many survival lessons. Angelou's early life was full of knocks and hardships.

There is a significant note in the closing words:

> See, you don't have to think about doing the right thing. If you're for the right thing, then you do it without thinking.

CHISHOLM, SHIRLEY. *Unbought and Unbossed.* Houghton Mifflin, 1970. Gr. 8–12*

In 1968, Shirley Chisholm became the first African American woman elected to the U.S. House of Representatives. She writes:

In a just and free society, it would be foolish [to gain fame for being Black and female rather than for one's accomplishments]. I hope if I am remembered it will finally be for what I have done, not for what I happen to be. And I hope that my having made it, the hard way, can be some kind of inspiration, particularly for women.

Written shortly after the 1968 election, this work is both an autobiography and a political manifesto—an exploration of Chisholm's path to Congress and her analysis of the challenges the country must meet to become just and free. She established a stronghold for African American candidates, unemployment insurance for domestic workers, and supported tenure rights for teachers whose pregnancy interrupted their careers. Elected four years later to the Ninety-first Congress, she emphasized jobs, job training, educational equity, adequate housing, enforcement of antidiscrimination laws, and support for day care.

She traces many of the problems to the schizophrenic birth of a country that paid eloquent tribute to "liberty and justice for all" while denying full rights of citizenship to African Americans and women.

EVANS, MARI. *I Am a Black Woman.* Morrow, 1970. Gr. 9–12.

Mari Evans's striking collection of poems explores the personal and political dimensions of being an African American woman. The exquisitely crafted and shaped poems affirm the Black woman's experiences of love, loneliness, pain, and "a black oneness, a black strength."

Using free verse and subtle rhymes, repetitive words and phrases, and evocative imagery, Evans explores the need for love and community. In tones of sadness, anger, defiance, and hope, she reaches for freedom from an oppressive society and from self-imposed constraints. She speaks of the need for reaching out for personal relationships. She applauds those who would seize collective power. And pervading all is her celebration of her African American identity.

GRAHAM, LORENZ. *Every Man Heart Lay Down.* Illustrated by Colleen Browning. Crowell, 1970. Gr. K–3.

When he served as ambassador to Liberia, Graham was most impressed by the rhythmic speech of the natives of that country. Listening to this kind of patois French that seemed to roll off the tongue, Graham was inspired to use it to write a group of biblical stories. One product of this endeavor was *Every Man Heart Lay Down*—a story that tells of God's plan to destroy his now evil-filled world. It is the story of his little "picayune" begging to be allowed to come into the world and save the people, a simple telling of the Christmas story when worshippers from afar come bringing gifts. Graham included the traditional gold and oil from the wise men, but in keeping with the story's setting, the "country people brought new rice . . . and every man heart lay down." *Every Man Heart Lay Down* is a timeless story written with a kind of poetic beauty and simplicity that begs to be read aloud.

GROSSMAN, BARNEY, WITH GLADYS GROOM AND THE PUPILS OF P.S. 150, THE BRONX, NEW YORK. *Black Means* . . . Illustrated by Charles Bible. Hill and Wang, 1970. Gr. K–3.

Gladys Groom was the teacher and Barney Grossman the principal at P.S. 150, an elementary school in a predominantly African American and Puerto Rican neighborhood. The two adults were concerned by the many negative connotations they felt were commonly associated with Blackness and began seeking positive images for their students—Black, Puerto Rican, and white. They first encouraged a dialogue at home and at school with the goal of developing a "thesaurus of positive images." A close look at the student-generated products spawned the idea of putting the words in a book—a format that would reach a wider audience. The final product was the award-winning *Black Means* . . . .

Charles Bible's graphic drawings—strong, positive, black-and-white images—give dramatic visual power to this beautiful and meaningful book.

JORDAN, JUNE, AND TERRI BUSH. *The Voice of the Children.* Holt, Rinehart, & Winston, 1970. Gr. 6–12.

To give the children a voice, the author June Jordan and then junior high school teacher Terri Bush organized a creative writing workshop in the Fort

Green section of Brooklyn. The children came voluntarily on Saturdays to "rap, dance, snack, browse among the books lying around, and write their stories, poems, editorials, and jokes." Out of those sessions grew a weekly magazine, *The Voice of the Children;* poetry readings; broadcasts; wider publication—and this volume of prose and poetry by twenty-five African American and Puerto Rican young people, ages nine to fifteen, whose photographs accompany June Jordan's afterword.

Michael Goode, age twelve, writes,

Some people talk in the hall
Some people talk in a drawl
Some people talk, talk, talk, talk
And never say anything at all.

But these young people have much to say about a world gone awry. They speak of loneliness, anger, pain, and the ultimate futility of hate.

But we are offered alternative visions as well, as in "Drums of Freedom," by Glen Thompson, age thirteen:

Some of us will die
but the drums will beat.
We may even lose but,
but the drums will beat.
They will beat loud and strong,
and
on
and
on
For we shall get what we want
and the drums will beat.

PETERS, MARGARET. *The Ebony Book of Black Achievement.* Johnson Publishing, 1970. Gr. 6–9*

As a high school teacher of English and American history, Peters was concerned about the dearth of information about African American history available to her students. She devoted her life to bringing information to the schools and to correcting distorted information. In this volume, she briefly sketches the lives of more than twenty Black men and women from the fourteenth through the twentieth centuries who distinguished themselves as inventors, explorers, revolutionaries, educators, abolitionists, and businesspeople, among other fields. Included are familiar names as well as others less frequently included in collective biographies, such as Granville Woods, whose air brake, induction telegraph, and third-rail system had a profound impact on American rail transportation. In brief sketches, Peters clearly presents her subjects' accomplishments, commitment, determination, and dedication to civilization.

UDRY, JANICE MAY. *Mary Jo's Grandmother.* Illustrated by Eleanor Mill. Whitman, 1970. Gr. K–3.

An early example of the cross-generation theme, Mary Jo visits her grandmother, who lives in the country. The activities in which Mary Jo and her family participate are the gentle things that speak of unhurried and stress-free time—learning how to sew, playing with the animals on the farm, making goodies in the kitchen under Grandmother's careful guidance, and acting very maturely when Grandmother has an accident.

　　This book is one in a series of Mary Jo stories. It might be reasonable to surmise that the Coretta Scott King awards jury selected it as an honor book to recognize a non-Black author for her sensitive treatment of a character from a minority culture.

1970 WINNER

PATTERSON, LILLIE. *Dr. Martin Luther King, Jr.: Man of Peace.* Illustrated with photographs. Garrard, 1969. Gr. K–3*

This book, written for young readers, is an introduction to the life of Martin Luther King Jr. and his nonviolent approach to achieving racial equality. The simply stated information and the timeliness of the book, published just after King's assassination, were among the factors that made this book the first title to receive the Coretta Scott King Book Award.

ILLUSTRATOR AWARDS
1974–2019

An * indicates nonfiction

2019 WINNER

BAUER, MARION DANE. *The Stuff of Stars.*
Illustrated by Ekua Holmes. Candlewick Press,
2018. Gr. Pre-K–3.

Few words can adequately express this book's
beauty and complexity. The images are lush,
bold, and vivid in telling of the complexity of
creation. Each successive page is uniquely different in its swirls of colors and bold strokes—
much like the universe itself. From the first
page to the last, Holmes's hand marbled paper and watercolor woodcut
illustrations provide an ocean of color. The combination of abstract patterns
and simple, amorphous figures keeps the reader enthralled throughout. The
illustrations help the reader imagine the possibility of merging science with
creating something from nothing. In the creation of the universe, the illustrations tell another story (or possibly a range of stories) that captures the
spirit of the African American experience through the infusion and inescap-

ability of the aesthetic that is unique to Holmes's technique. Holmes is captivatingly brilliant in bringing the beginning of life to a crescendo. —*Sujin Huggins*

2019 HONORS

SHETTERLY, MARGOT LEE. *Hidden Figures: The True Story of Four Black Women and the Space Race.* **Illustrated by Laura Freeman.** Harper: an imprint of HarperCollins Publishers, 2018. Gr. Pre-K–3*

Freeman's stylistic and expressive illustrations pair exceptionally well with Shetterly's expository text about four unsung African American women pioneers of the space race movement of the 1950s and 1960s. In this picture-book version of Shetterly's 2016 award-winning book for adults, Freeman gives the reader a realistic glimpse into history with illustrations that make these historical women leap right off the page. The contributions of Dorothy Vaughan, Mary Jackson, Katherine Johnson, and Christine Darden are fashionably brought to life with vibrant and crisp illustrations, enhanced by mathematical equations that encourage readers to reach for the stars. The bright, bold illustrations celebrate this daring and adventurous group of women who broke the glass ceilings and racial barriers in a time of segregation. —*Christina Vortia*

CLARK-ROBINSON, MONICA. *Let the Children March.* **Illustrated by Frank Morrison.** Houghton Mifflin Harcourt, 2018. Gr. 1-4*

While there are many books about the Children's Crusade in Birmingham, Alabama, *Let the Children March* is notable in that it truly captures the emotions, the inspiration, the brutality, the significance, and the triumph of the march, and it does so largely through Morrison's illustrations. From opening pages that foreground the wire fence demarcating the playground for "whites only" to a very different view in the closing pages of that fence, which now features the sign "park," welcoming the very children it sought to exclude, Morrison takes the reader on a visually profound journey of depth—both in color and insight—in a realistic style that is all too real. A fine addition to civil rights literature for children. —*Sujin Huggins*

DUNCAN, ALICE FAYE. *Martin, Memphis, and the Mountaintop: The Sanitation Strike of 1968.* Illustrated by R. Gregory Christie. Calkins Creek: an imprint of Highlights, 2018. Gr. 3–6*

This story of the Sanitation Strike of 1968 in Memphis follows nine-year-old Lorraine, whose father participates in the protest. Christie's use of color, composition, light, and nuance effectively captures the humanity, urgency, loss, and triumph of an important part of African American history. Christie varies composition and style in amazing ways in this somewhat genre-defying book. The soft, buttery yellows throughout the text are offset with subtle blues and occasional bold slashes of warmer dark pinks. Christie's deceptively simple illustrations perfectly complement this narrative of an overlooked moment in the Civil Rights Movement. —*Irene Briggs*

2019 JOHN STEPTOE NEW TALENT AWARD

MORA, OGE. *Thank You, Omu!* Illustrated by Oge Mora. Little, Brown and Company, 2018. Gr. Pre-S–3.

A fresh take on a timeless tale of altruism and community-mindedness, this delicious concoction of text, illustrations, and design is vibrant, colorful, and full of child appeal. It evokes images of an idyllic multicultural community where everyone is your neighbor. While this may not be reminiscent of all communities, the imagery is suggestive of the type of community that Martin Luther King Jr. dreamed about and that others have paid for with their lives. Mora's collage work is skillfully pieced together with acrylic, marker, pastels, patterned paper, and old book clippings—a visual smorgasbord of warmth. The varied fonts for the "knocks" and "Thank you, Omu!"s flow so well on each and every spread, bringing to life a figure that is an amalgamation of many grandmothers and captures the African spirit of generosity and community. —*Jessica Anne Bratt*

2018 WINNER

ALEXANDER, KWAME, WITH CHRIS COLDER-LEY AND MARJORY WENTWORTH. *Out of Wonder: Poems Celebrating Poets.* **Illustrated by Ekua Holmes.** Candlewick Press, 2017. Gr. 3–5*

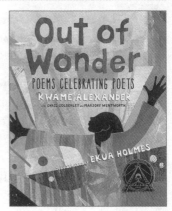

Out of Wonder is a collection of poetry that features the work of various poets from diverse cultures, such as Emily Dickinson, Walter Dean Myers, and Basho, just to name a few. Holmes's colorful, vibrant, collages are full of texture. Combine the techniques with Holmes' choice of lively earth tones—the fusion of all of these techniques reflects those of African American art. Her illustrations pay homage to the Black Art aesthetic and beautifully pull together this eclectic collection of poetry. Simply beautiful. Short biographies of the poets can be found at the end. *—LaKeshia N. Darden*

2018 HONORS

BARNES, DERRICK. *Crown: An Ode to the Fresh Cut.* **Illustrated by Gordon C. James.** Bolden Books/Agate Publishing, 2017. Gr. 2–5.

The empowering, nearly magical effects of a good haircut are celebrated in Barnes's jubilant free verse and James's joyous, spirited oil paintings. Their Black barbershop is bursting with the pride of men and boys (and even one woman) taking pleasure in their cool and culture together. Barnes brings us into the boy's thoughts as he speculates about smashing his geography test or impressing the girls at school the next day while wearing his fresh, new, tight fade. James's loose, easy brushstrokes are as smooth as jazz as he shifts our focus from the interior of the shop to the heads of its fly patrons. Whether the customers have selected to have designs shaved into their scalps or sport a faux-hawk, dreadlocks, or cornrows, each is clearly destined to walk out the door with swagger and self-confidence. You're never too young or too old to "leave out of 'the shop' every single time, feeling the exact same way . . . Magnificent. Flawless. Like royalty." *—Miriam Lang Budin*

CLINE-RANSOME, LESA. *Before She Was Harriet.* Illustrated by James E. Ransome. Holiday House, 2017. Pre-K–2*

Before She Was Harriet is a beautiful and unique picture book biography poetically written and illustrated about the legendary Harriet Tubman. Popularly known as "Moses" or "General Tubman," she was also known by other names throughout her remarkable life. Readers learn, through a lyrical reverse chronology, that before she was Harriet, she was first Araminta and then Minty as a child. Later, she was Aunt Harriet, a nurse, and a spy for the Union Army.

The story ends with a return to the main character in old age after she chooses her final name, Harriet. This book provides a rare and refreshing perspective of one of the most significant fabled figures in American history. —*Nichole Shabazz*

2018 JOHN STEPTOE NEW TALENT AWARD

ERSKINE, KATHRYN. *Mama Africa! How Miriam Makeba Spread Hope with Her Song.* Illustrated by Charly Palmer. Farrar, Straus and Giroux, 2017. Gr. 4–6*

Erskine chronicles the remarkable life of Miriam Makeba, a courageous and renowned singer, musician, and spirit who used her gift of song to protest and bring attention to the racial injustices of apartheid or the separation of Blacks and whites in her country of South Africa. Racial inequality and unrest, fueled by the system of apartheid, loom large throughout the story of Makeba's notable life in the struggle for freedom, yet her music and the message it sends to her people propel them forward.

Palmer's colorful portraits provide the perfect visual while depicting the beautiful struggle endured by Makeba and the Black people of South Africa as they resisted racial injustice. Using her music and songs as a rallying cry for righteousness, Makeba exposes apartheid and the racism of South Africa on the world stage. As the whole world listens, her voice gets stronger and louder, like a lion's roar, and Miriam Makeba is transformed into Mama Africa, a lyrical lioness who bravely lived, in service and song, for equal justice and freedom for all. —*Nichole Shabazz*

2017 WINNER

STEPTOE, JAVAKA. *Radiant Child: The Story of Young Artist Jean-Michel Basquiat.* Illustrated by Javaka Steptoe. Little, Brown and Company, 2016. Gr. 2–5*

Steptoe's stunning homage to Basquiat breaks new ground in the realm of the picture book. In a note opposite the title page, Steptoe describes the manner in which he "painted on richly texture pieces of found wood." The resulting illustrations seamlessly blend Basquiat's style with that of the author/illustrator. Steptoe echoes the bold colors, thick lines, and messy quality of Basquiat's work (to borrow from Steptoe's text: "His drawings are not neat or clean, nor does he color inside the lines. They are sloppy, ugly, and sometimes weird; but somehow still beautiful."). Steptoe seems to have a deep understanding of what Basquiat was trying to do with his art, and he apparently intended to help readers develop an understanding and appreciation of Basquiat's talents and contributions. His mission was successful. —*Sam Bloom*

2017 HONORS

BRYAN, ASHLEY. *Freedom Over Me: Eleven Slaves, Their Lives and Dreams Brought to Life by Ashley Bryan.* Illustrated by Ashley Bryan. Atheneum/ Caitlyn Dlouhy Books, 2016. Gr. 4–6.

Using pen, ink, watercolors, and historical documents, Ashley Bryan depicts "the pains, the sufferings" and trauma endured by daughters and sons of African tribes enslaved in America, capturing the reality of an oppressive institution that must remain visible, lest one forget. Readers should not misconstrue any "smiles" on the eleven faces, as the expressions come from resistance, not subservience, to white America.

On alternating pages, Bryan's characters express joy only when discussing their dreams. "Dream" pages project color and depth, while full-face illustrations for lived experiences are deliberately flat. These stoic close-ups—featuring subdued tones and a collage background—show the strength needed to endure their existence. Radiant expressions on the dream pages depict pride, and the diverse melanin tones indicate many origins, reminding us the characters descend from queens and kings from ancestral lands.

The atrocities committed against Qush, sixty-two, through the youngest, Dora, eight, are a reminder of the roots of the United States. The images reflect the past—"a long trail of years/flushed with tears"—and the present: freedom is still not achieved. —*Omobolade Delano-Oriarian, Suzanne Fondrie, and Marguerite Penick-Parks*

WEATHERFORD, CAROLE BOSTON. *Freedom in Congo Square.* Illustrated by R. Gregory Christie. Little Bee Books, 2016. Gr. 2–5*

Using rhyming couplets, Weatherford narrates enslaved people's week from "Mondays, there were hogs to slop /mules to train, and logs to chop" through their one afternoon when "They flocked to New Orleans' Congo Square." The couplets simplify but by no means purify the backbreaking and dehumanizing work of enslaved men and women. Everything about this book, from the stylized cover image dancing on streets ironically paved with gold to the brilliant Tuscany yellow endpapers, tells the story of pain and hardship mixed with anticipation of time shared with friends and relatives in Congo Square. Christie's angular figures, painted with a single tear but few other identifying features, reveal the pain of "dreaded lash" while anticipating "four more days to Congo Square." When the enslaved men and women finally flock to their Sunday afternoon of temporary freedom, Christie's art reveals fully formed bodies and faces in a ballet of praise. The final lines of the poem reveal the rejoicing and carefree companionship of enslaved people on Sunday afternoons, "half day, half free in Congo Square . . . freedom's heart." Foreword and back matter provide historical background to the story. —*Linda M. Pavonetti*

JACKSON, RICHARD. *In Plain Sight.* Illustrated by Jerry Pinkney. Roaring Brook Press, 2016. Gr. K–3.

Sophie and Grandpa play a game every day after school. Grandpa, confined to a wheelchair, finds ways to hide everyday meaningful items from his life for Sophie to find. Readers can spot each hidden item before Sophie does with her eagle eyes. The close relationship between the generations is matched with the richness of the colored pencil and watercolor illustrations.

Pinkney's warm signature style depicts this African American family in a multigenerational household. When Sophie turns the tables on Grandpa, even the ever-present cat is in on the fun. Details here are plentiful, illustrating Grandpa's current interests, as well as the richness of his past history, while hiding each special object. This slice of present-day life depicts a loving family and the simple joys connecting and enriching their lives.
—*Carol Edwards*

2016 WINNER

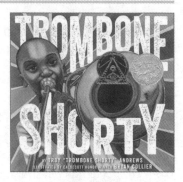

ANDREWS, TROY, AND BILL TAYLOR.
Trombone Shorty. **Illustrated by Bryan Collier.**
Abrams, 2015. Gr. 3–5*

Where y'at? Troy Andrews, aka Trombone Shorty, uses this greeting to invite readers into life in Tremé, the New Orleans neighborhood where he grew up. In Tremé, he was immersed in music; becoming a musician seemed the natural thing to do. Andrews's rendering of his life story is perfectly complemented and richly enhanced by Bryan Collier's watercolor and collage illustrations. Collier captures the spirit of the city and the vibrancy of its ubiquitous music with bright colors and shapes that emanate from Troy's trombone as well as the colorful balloons that float over the city like musical notes. Using a variety of perspectives, Collier's illustrations create an artistic gumbo that reflects the rhythms and energy of the city and its music, and, in a sense, its signature dish. Both the story of Trombone Shorty's devotion to his music and the illustrations that brilliantly reflect that life story are an inspiration to readers young and old. Back matter includes an author's note, an illustrator's note, a photo of Andrews, and information on his foundation.
—*Rudine Sims Bishop*

2016 HONORS

MICHEAUX NELSON, VAUNDA. *The Book Itch: Freedom, Truth & Harlem's Greatest Bookstore.* **Illustrated by R. Gregory Christie.** Carolrhoda Books, 2015. Gr. 2–4*

Nelson and Christie return to the National Memorial African Bookstore in Harlem in their second profile of Lewis Michaux, the author's great-uncle. This one, told through the eyes of Lewis Jr., son of the bookstore's iconic owner, appeals to a younger crowd than the author/illustrator duo's earlier *No Crystal Stair.* Christie's richly textured illustrations feature broad brush strokes and nods to the colors of the Pan-African flag and books themselves. His use of straight lines, such as on the front cover, creates myriad boxes in the art to create numerous book-like shapes, fitting in with the story's bookstore setting and the importance of books to the storyline. Christie's expressionist art style not only captures the time period perfectly, but also facial expressions, such as looks of awe when Muhammad Ali visits the bookstore and sadness and despair when Malcolm X is shot. Coupled with an engaging narrative from Nelson, *The Book Itch* is an exemplary historical picture book. —*Sam Bloom*

DE LA PEÑA, MATT. *Last Stop on Market Street.* **Illustrated by Christian Robinson.** G. P. Putnam's Sons, 2015. Pre-K–2.

A weekly outing following church services on Sundays is the backdrop for this award-winning story by Matt de la Peña, with illustrations by Christian Robinson. On the weekly trip, CJ has lots of questions for his nana. He seems frustrated and unhappy that they do not have a car and take the bus in the rain. He resents not being able to play with his friends, envies the riders on the bus who have iPods, and wonders why their trip takes them to a dirty part of the city. In reply, his grandmother poses questions for CJ. With her wisdom and experience, she helps CJ see beauty in the world around him and gain a new appreciation for what is truly important in the world.

This endearing story highlights the love between a grandmother and her grandson, seeing the world through the eyes of a child and the importance of looking beyond ourselves to meet the needs of others. —*Ida W. Thompson*

2015 WINNER

COPELAND, MISTY. *Firebird.* Illustrated by Christopher Myers. G. P. Putnam's Sons, 2014. Gr. K–3*

Cultural authenticity, relevance, persistence, and Black herstory emanate from Misty Copeland's poetry and Christopher Myers's layered painted collages. The warm reds, yellows, and confident oranges are filled with movement in this extraordinary story about the power of learning to believe in oneself amid odds or racial barriers. Copeland, the second African American soloist with the American Ballet Theatre, offers a dialogue between herself and a young girl who, despite racial limitations, persists and finds her way to dance.

Copeland sweeps away the young dancer's clouds of doubt: "darling child, don't you know / you're just where I started / let the sun shine on your face / your beginning's just begun." Myers deconstructs tokenism, as his illustrations authentically depict Misty's beautiful ebony skin. Her hair pulled into an authentic bun of a Black dancer, avoids the white hegemonic practice of the "image of what a ballerina should be . . . with tendrils sweeping her face."

Copeland and Myers conclude *Firebird* by offering diverse images of children immersed in the beauty of ballet revealing to children that anything is possible. —*Omobolade Delano-Oriarian, Suzanne Fondrie, and Marguerite W. Penick-Parks*

2015 HONORS

POWELL, PATRICIA HRUBY. *Josephine: The Dazzling Life of Josephine Baker.* Illustrated by Christian Robinson. Chronicle Books, 2014. Gr. 4*

Josephine Baker was no ordinary dancer and certainly no ordinary woman in 1920's America. Her exotic dance styles and costumes made her world renowned, yet she met with discrimination at every turn in the United States, her home country. She was determined and fearless as she went about transforming dance during that time period. Powell's fluid, poetic style describes Baker's life with sophisticated, emotional language, using the format of performing arts. Quotations by Baker add depth and realism to this picture-book biography. Robinson's simplistic, spot-on illustrative portrayal of Baker shows her regal demeanor and fluid movements that give the dancer a larger-than-life feel. At times, she seems to be floating on the page. Author and illustrator notes, bibliography, and photo credits are included. —*Christina Dorr*

RUSSELL-BROWN, KATHERYN. *Little Melba and Her Big Trombone.* Illustrated by Frank Morrison. Lee & Low, 2014. Gr. 1–3*

Bright, rich colors and a flowing cartoon style tell the story of Little Melba Doretta Liston in this amazing picture book. Music flows throughout the text and illustrations in this true story. As Little Melba learns to play her big trombone, Grandpa John instructs her in ways to cradle and stretch to accommodate her instrument. Young readers will almost hear and feel the rhythm of the sounds in the text as they enjoy the detailed pictures. Morrison's use of perspective and framing clearly show the ups and downs of Melba's tale of triumph and ultimate success. —*April Roy*

2014 WINNER

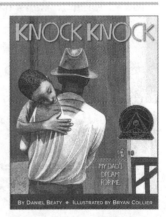

BEATY, DANIEL. *Knock Knock: My Dad's Dream for Me.* Illustrated by Bryan Collier. Little, Brown, 2013. Gr. Pre-K–2.

Beginning with the title page, the earth tones of the city contrast vividly with a bright blue sky of pieces of paper expertly woven together, suggesting that anything is possible on such a beautiful day. The story begins with a young boy waiting for his father to wake him in the morning. He and his father play a game called Knock Knock. The father knocks on his son's bedroom door every morning and tells him that he loves him. One day the knock doesn't come and the son is left to wonder where his father is. The father doesn't return and the young son soon becomes a young man.

Beaty and Collier are true partners in this timely work. Beaty's sparse but somber text meshes beautifully with Collier's abundant landscape of texture and color. The pairing in the message of the longing for a parent with the strength and resiliency of a child is handled with extraordinary care.

2014 HONOR

NELSON, KADIR. *Nelson Mandela.* Illustrated by Kadir Nelson. Katherine Tegen Books, 2013. Gr. 2–5*

Kadir Nelson illustrates the life of Nelson Mandela from child to president with powerful and beautiful paintings. His verse is a narrative about segregation and protest in South African history. The young reader will easily enjoy and identify with some of the images, such as stick fighting, the young Nelson being consoled by his mother, and the joyful older Nelson newly elected as president of South Africa. Other illustrations and verse should inspire questions and may require further explanations because some concepts may be unfamiliar, such as the role of ancestors in South African cultures. Also, even at their young lives, young readers may be acquainted with unfairness and can identify real-life injustices within their communities and will therefore need further explanations to better understand what lay behind the political activism in the decades-long struggle for freedom in South Africa. There is much that children can learn from Nelson Mandela's life, and Kadir Nelson's paintings are a visual contribution to the story of his life and history.

2014 JOHN STEPTOE AWARD FOR NEW TALENT

HILL, LABAN CARRICK. *When the Beat Was Born: DJ Kool Herc and the Creation of Hip Hop.* Illustrated by Theodore Taylor III. Roaring Brook Press, 2013. Gr. 2–4*

It was in Kingston, Jamaica, that Clive first experienced music pulsating through big speakers at neighborhood block parties. When his family moved to New York City, Clive carried his love of the sound with him. When his dad brought home really big speakers, Clive's longing to create the big sound moved from entertaining the neighbors to creating the bebop sound of street parties. Morphing into the persona of DJ Kool Herc, Clive added the twist of two turntables to expand the dancing experience. This was the introduction to break dancing, gymnastic moves that remain popular today. His use of two turntables is still *the* technique used by DJ's to keep the dancing going. While Hill's words capture the story, it is Taylor's illustrations that go beyond by utilizing movement and a kaleidoscope of color that gives the visual sense of DJ Kool's sound.

2013 WINNER

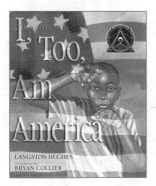

HUGHES, LANGSTON. *I, Too, Am America*. Illustrated by Bryan Collier. Simon & Schuster, 2012. Gr. K–4.

A young African American boy peeks through the stripes on an iconic American flag for the cover of *I, Too, Am America*. Before one has even cracked the spine of this powerful work, the beauty of the boy and his steadfast look of determination over the word "America" make a powerful statement spanning hundreds of years in a single image. Collier's collage rendering of Langston Hughes's 1925 poem, "I, Too" is set on fast-moving trains traversing the United States. Pullman porters, a group of African American men, worked the railways in the late nineteenth to mid-twentieth centuries. Known for their level of service and dedication, the Porters helped educate others along their railway lines by taking discarded passenger items such as newspapers or records and distributing them to those without access.

Collier uses his gift of collage to carry the metaphor of the discarded Pullman newspapers from the past to the present. Pieces of the American flag float through time and place to land on characters' faces and landscapes—a subtle reminder that we are all America.

2013 HONORS

LYONS, KELLY STARLING. *Ellen's Broom*. Illustrated by Daniel Minter. G. P. Putnam's Sons, 2012. Gr. K–3.

Daniel Minter captures the sweetness of romantic love, family, and community in his hand-painted linoleum blocks. Bright pinks, blues, and purples and warm golden yellows bring movement to a technique that is often thought of as stiff and emotionless. In Kelly Lyons's tale of a family during Reconstruction, Minter's characters leap off the page as they worship in church and celebrate the fact that all marriages can now be legally registered. Just as powerful are the pages that illustrate the family discussions of slavery. Minter uses sepia tones to denote the past. The facial expressions clearly demonstrate loss as family, friends, and lovers are ripped apart. However, the sepia tones also express joy as Papa and Mama jump the broom. Minter's linoleum block technique suggests forward movement into a hopeful future. His illustrations truly extend the text, reflecting the warmth of family and community and the hopefulness of the future that will always be grounded in tradition.

MYERS, CHRISTOPHER. *H.O.R.S.E.: A Game of Basketball and Imagination.* Egmont, 2012. Gr. K–5.

In *H.O.R.S.E.,* Christopher Myers mixes photo collage and two painted figures, elongated TALL guys who aren't just using their height to take their shots with a bright orange basketball. As the two friends prepare their shots with long, long arms ready to compete, their words take over the game, and it morphs into a boast-fest of one fantastic shot after another. As their game goes stratospheric, and possibly even intergalactic, the text leaps from its confines and curves overhead and around planets.

Myers's page-spanning paintings even feature a guest appearance by Hayden Planetarium Director Neil deGrasse Tyson, who points to the path of the "new basketball-shaped comet." Young readers may or may not get this visual joke or Myers's note, which is a tribute to an artist friend who is bonded to Myers by history, imagination, and athleticism. However, Myers is exactly on young readers' wavelength in the two players' one-upmanship, and boys of all ages will undoubtedly relish the fantastical tongue dunk. His players inhabit free and expansive blank spaces until their ball takes off for outer space. The sparse use of photos of formal earthbound city buildings provides contrast to the free-flowing paintings and text.

KING, MARTIN LUTHER, JR. *I Have a Dream: Martin Luther King, Jr.* **Illustrated by Kadir Nelson.** Schwartz and Wade Books/Random House Children's Books, 2012. Gr. K–5.

Kadir Nelson's signature oil paintings bring the moment of the *I Have a Dream* speech to life as well as a variety of less specific (but not less powerful) moments. This abbreviated version of the speech somewhat limits the scope of the picture book itself. However, readers can listen to the entire speech that is available on an enclosed CD contained in the back matter. The excerpted speech enabled Nelson to pair images with particular sentiments. He created a unique version with emphasis placed on Dr. King's stature, spirituality, and sustained memory. The pictures vary in terms of focus and layout. Double-page spreads create a sense of place (long view from the reflecting pool), for dramatic emphasis (white and black hands clasped), and to add a personal face to the struggle, a family portrait. The striking realism and rich colors will draw readers in and keep their attention.

2012 WINNER

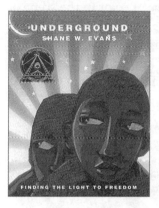

EVANS, SHANE W. *Underground: Finding the Light to Freedom.* Roaring Brook Press, 2011. Gr. 2–6.

While it can be a fairly exhausting task to consider the intricacies and hardships of the Underground Railroad, it takes a fair amount of genius to explain it to young children. Shane Evans has created a wonderful introduction to this complex system in his book *Underground.* With sparse text and evocative striking images, Evans describes the dangerous and desperate journey of a group of slaves as they travel through the endless nights, looking up to the stars and moon to guide the way to freedom. Skillful use of perspective helps convey the movement of the Underground Railroad through a muted palette of dark blues that gives way to progressively brighter tones on double-spread pages. Taking the most harrowing of conditions and condensing them into succinct yet powerful statements, Evans tells a story understood by audiences of all ages.

2012 HONOR

NELSON, KADIR. *Heart and Soul: The Story of America and African Americans.* Balzer & Bray, 2011. Gr. 3–7*

Heart and Soul is like a treasured family photograph album that captures the highlights and heartaches of African American history. An elder African American "Everywoman" tells the story of her life and America's history. The reader will linger over the full-page illustrations and double-page spreads in this oversized book. Kadir Nelson's stunning oil paintings portray bold images of known and unknown historical personalities. The portrait of a nameless African American Revolutionary War soldier is just as powerful as the one of abolitionist Frederick Douglass. The sepia-toned picture of a young girl in a vintage oval picture frame and one of a well-dressed 1920's Harlem couple are striking enlarged reproductions of the studio photographs of that era. Nelson has selectively chosen to illustrate pivotal events in African American history. The determination on the faces of the men depicted in the labor strike picture captures the spirit of activism in the African American community. The dramatic use of color in the scene of a blazing burning cross is a contrast to the close-up of the hands of a senior citizen holding an "I voted" button. As the narrator says, "You have to know where you come from so you can move forward." Children and teens will be attracted to this book's vivid illustrations that show them the past and promise a bright future.

2011 WINNER

HILL, LABAN CARRICK. *Dave the Potter.* Illustrated by Bryan Collier. Little, Brown, 2010. Gr. K–3*

A picture-book homage to a strong, brilliant artist, Collier uses his own prodigious talent to bring the life of Dave the Potter to young readers. Using collage and earth-toned paints, Collier both reveres and respects the artist whose works still amaze potters today. In the foreground of many spreads, we see Dave working in "mud pie heaven," while the background honestly shows the life of a slave. He is an artist who refuses to allow his lack of freedom to stop him from being an artist. The image of Dave standing in front of the tree, with it seemingly growing out of his head, includes family images in the branches. The play of light and shadow, particularly on Dave's hands, arms, and clothing, gives the illustrations depth and power. Emotional without being didactic, Collier gets the details of the craft right—the caked palms, the dry, chapped skin, tongue-thrusted concentration, the magical moment when a round of wedged clay becomes a perfectly centered pot. This is a book that is like one of Dave's pots—at first glance, simple to look at, but, upon inspection, centered and filled with power.

2011 HONOR

GOLIO, GARY. *Jimi: Sounds Like a Rainbow: A Story of the Young Jimi Hendrix.* Illustrated by Javaka Steptoe. Clarion Books, 2010. Gr. 3–5*

"Electricity ripped through the air . . . Jimmy's hand jumped, and a rainbow of color pencils went tumbling to the floor . . . Jimmy grabbed his one-string ukulele. He could play only simple tunes, but now he had a new idea . . . to paint pictures with sound."

When Jimmy received a second-hand guitar, it broadened his musical ingenuity. Later, Jimmy acquired an electric guitar and amplifiers. "He learned to use it as an artist uses paint, creating new worlds with the colors of sound."

Gary Golio's lyrical text sets the tone of the story at the very beginning. Using words that have musical connotations like "electricity," "pound," and "rock" immediately thrusts young readers into Jimmy's musical world. Golio focuses on Jimmy's music and artistic talents rather than his impoverished life. Javaka Steptoe's illustrations match perfectly with Golio's text and Jimmy's story. On each page, Jimmy is in the forefront, listening, drawing, dreaming, and playing until the very end of the story. An author's note provides a list of resources.

2011 JOHN STEPTOE NEW TALENT AWARD

JOHNSON, JEN CULLERTON. *Seeds of Change.* Illustrated by Sonia Lynn Sadler. Lee & Low, 2010. Gr. 2–4*

Seeds of Change is a picture book biography of Wangari Maathai, Kenyan women's activist, environmentalist, scientist, and Nobel Laureate. Her mother instilled Wangari's love of learning and nature in her as a young girl. She treasured trees, valued them as a food source, and promised never to cut them down. Although it was not customary for Kenyan girls to be educated, her parents decided to send her to school. Wangari went to America to study science and learned that, even as a woman, she could accomplish whatever she set her mind to. Returning home to Kenya, she founded the Green Belt Movement, changing the country's landscape and ultimately spreading the message of planting trees and caring for the environment around the world.

Wangari's life of devotion to protecting the natural world she loved serves as an example to young readers of how one person can inspire others to appreciate and care for the environment. Illustrator Sonia Lynn Sadler's vivid, bright colors and textures infuse vibrancy into this biography with every turn of the page.

2010 WINNER

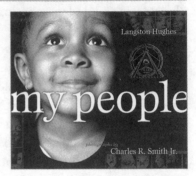

HUGHES, LANGSTON. *My People.* **Illustrated by Charles R. Smith Jr.** Atheneum Books for Young Readers, 2009. Gr. Pre-K–3.

Bold, antiqued, sepia-toned photographs that accompany and complement one of Langston Hughes's most memorable poems define this stunning book. Each page is a celebration of African American people of all ages, colors, and hues. Whether the subject is laughing, thinking, dancing, or crying, each page pops with emotion and celebration of the beauty and variety of African American people. The sophisticated design employs typefaces of varying sizes, emphasizing each word of this thirty-three-word masterpiece. Adding to the rhythm and pacing, Smith includes lightly shaded filmstrip-like photos along the edges of most spreads. Smith's eye for detail and his extraordinary photographs eloquently express the pride and love the poet felt for his people, capturing equally the curiosity and excitement of youth and the experience and wisdom of elders. This is the first time photography has been honored by the committee.

2010 HONOR

HUGHES, LANGSTON. *The Negro Speaks of Rivers.* **Illustrated by E. B. Lewis.** Disney/Jump at the Sun, 2009. Gr. K–8.

In Hughes's classic poem, brief language is deceptively simple; a deep current of emotion rises to the surface through Lewis's beautifully painted images of people and waters in pastoral shades of blue, green, and gold. The juxtaposition of the majestic, wide waterway with the earthy, quotidian portrait of hands and pot set the theme for this volume: rivers represent a continuum of life, and, in particular here, African American life throughout history. Some rivers significant to this history are named: "I bathed in the Euphrates when dawns were young. / I built my hut near the Congo and it lulled me to sleep." Some of the paintings are realistic, including a charming image of a man and a boy fishing on the banks of the Mississippi; others are more spiritual, such as a self-portrait of Lewis himself (identified as such in an illustrator's note), shown praying against a backdrop of dark green, presumably deep water with rippling lines flowing across a stylized depiction of his upper body. Written in 1920, this poem remains relevant and eloquent, especially as interpreted through Lewis's affecting watercolors.

2009 WINNER

THOMAS, JOYCE CAROL. *The Blacker the Berry: Poems.* Illustrated by Floyd Cooper. HarperCollins, 2008. Gr. 3–6.

Songwriters, poets, and authors often refer to the color black as if it were one dark density: "Black is the color of my true love's hair"; "Out of the night that covers me, / Black as the Pit from pole to pole"; "I am a Negro, black as the night is black." Artist Floyd Cooper captures all the nuances of the color in perfect response to Thomas's words. There's Grandma drinking coffee so thick and black "a spoon could stand in it"; the "biscuit brown" face of a young boy; a girl, dark skin contrasting with her bright yellow dress, who realizes that it's the dark of night that makes a bright dawn possible; and the smiling, red-haired child, whose face looks almost white, who is proud of the single drop of blood that makes her Black. Cooper's closing painting, a multicultural gathering of children of all shades of black, extends Thomas's message that every shade of black is beautiful.

2009 HONORS

NELSON, KADIR. *We Are the Ship: The Story of Negro League Baseball.* Jump at the Sun/Hyperion Books for Children, 2008. Gr. 3–8*

Kadir Nelson captures the spirit of Negro League Baseball in *We Are the Ship*. With artistic realism, he takes us back and makes time stand still. His elegant, up-close renderings of players, such as Raleigh "Biz" Mackey and

Wilber "Bullet" Rogan, or of players standing in dappled sunlight (Leroy "Satchel" Paige in Yankee Stadium), bring to life the human drama of these often forgotten athletes and their contributions to our great national pastime. Nelson captures the seduction of the night game with halos of light against a great dark sky, miniaturizing the players as if to signify the monumental obstacles encountered by these determined African Americans. The gatefold showcasing the players of the first Colored World Series in 1924, at Muehlebach Field in Kansas City, Missouri, is a stunning example of the scope of the artist's talent. Each of the forty-one players is different. Deep, rich color fills the other single- and double-page spreads as well. All are enhanced by a brilliant use of light, accented by an occasional pale blue sky. Nelson brings the players and the game to life with sensitivity and reverence.

ASTON, DIANNA HUTTS. *The Moon Over Star.* Illustrated by Jerry Pinkney. Dial, 2008. Gr. Pre-K–3.

As Mae's grandpa leads the singing in church, Mae is thinking of the Apollo 11 astronauts who are about to land on the moon. Jerry Pinkney's pencil, ink, and watercolor illustrations allow readers to experience the enormity of the historic event while identifying with Mae's dream of joining the space program. Pinkney has a distinguished history of depicting space travel. His experience is evident throughout this book as he moves readers back and forth between the historical images and scenes from Mae's warm world— her father giving her a reassuring embrace, her friends building a makeshift rocket from wheels, ladders, and barrels found in the barn. The double-page spread of the fiery Apollo takeoff is balanced by the wonder of Mae's family staring up at the sky while enjoying an evening picnic. In a black-and-white spread suggestive of the television broadcast watched by 600 million people around the world, Pinkney depicts the astronauts cavorting on the surface of the moon. The closing image of the astronauts' footsteps on the lunar surface invites Mae (and readers) to fill those shoes.

WEATHERFORD, CAROLE BOSTON. *Before John Was a Jazz Giant: A Song of John Coltrane.* Illustrated by Sean Qualls. Henry Holt, 2008. Gr. K–3.

Carole Boston Weatherford's brief text describes the musical influences that shaped the life of the renowned jazz saxophonist John Coltrane. Coltrane grew up in High Point, North Carolina, where "he heard hambones knocking in Grandma's pots, / Daddy strumming the ukulele / . . . Mama playing hymns for the senior choir / . . . and a saxophone's soulful solo, / blue notes crooning his name." Painting in acrylics and using collage and pencil accents, Sean Qualls illustrates the picture-book tribute with a muted, harmonious palette of blue, brown, terra-cotta, and black. Floating notes, bubbles, and ribbons of sound evoke the rhythmic world that shaped this musical great. The paint-saturated pages combine representational images with abstract shapes, beautifully reflecting Coltrane's music, which surrounded listeners with riffs on familiar melodies.

2009 JOHN STEPTOE NEW TALENT AWARD

ELLIOTT, ZETTA. *Bird.* Illustrated by Shadra Strickland. Lee & Low, 2008. Gr. 2–5.

Although he's still struggling with his grandfather's death, Mehkai (nicknamed Bird by Granddad) realizes that he and his family suffer even more from the death of drug-addicted Marcus, Bird's older brother. The illustrations, a combination of gouache, watercolor, pencil, and charcoal, carry a heavy emotional load, but Strickland's palette, mostly muted grays, blues, and browns, conveys the reflective mood with a lightness of touch. Uncle Son, Granddad's friend, is mentoring Bird, providing him with words of comfort and encouraging him to practice his drawing, revel in his love of birds, and develop his "own special something" that will help him soar. Lines drawn in soft gray pencil accompany the more realistic depictions of characters and events, balancing the hard facts of life with an imagined world. Grief haunts each picture, but there's a surprising uplifting quality in the close relationship between the boy and the adult who serves as his support. Strickland's careful use of light and dark (hope and despair) turns the sensitive poetry into a visual jazz riff that honors both the reality of Bird's life and his feelings and thoughts.

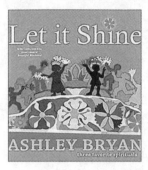

2008 WINNER

BRYAN, ASHLEY. *Let It Shine: Three Favorite Spirituals.* Atheneum, 2007. Gr. K–3.

When does a stack of brightly colored papers become a wondrous work of art? It happens when the skilled fingers and creative imagination of Ashley Bryan converge. The result is an image-filled collage giving brilliant visual interpretation to the artist's best-loved spirituals. The ingenious use of the media of collage invites the reader to scrutinize each illustration for those details that add dimension to the seemingly simple words. In the first selection, each "little light" is different, from the candle to the lantern to a flashlight and others. The smoothly turned curves in the double-page spread of the mother cuddling her child convey the sense of comfort and security that says He truly holds "the little bitty baby in His hands." Tambourines, drums, maracas, and myriad musical instruments provide a visual rhythmic beat as "the Saints go marching in." The universal appeal of this musical form captures the clearly definable multicultural personalities pictured on the pages. Memory-filled sewing shears and embroidery scissors inherited from the artist's mother cut each well-thought-out scene.

2008 HONORS

JOY, N. *The Secret Olivia Told Me.* **Illustrated by Nancy Devard.** Just Us Books, 2007. Gr. K–3.

With a limited color palette of black, white, gray, bright red, and brick tones, Devard's illustrations of shape, line, and color illustrate a story that opens with a heart-to-heart conversation and ends with a dramatic explosion. Devard depicts the story using silhouettes, which appear at once shadowy and rock solid. This technique recalls the creation of that art form in the work of the African American artist Kara Walker. Children in action, passing along stories not meant for other ears, and a bright red balloon hovering with its string trailing through the air symbolize a tale told from mouth to ear, from cell phone to cell phone, even on the playground. These are among the striking images of friendship almost broken—even as the red balloon explodes. Clever use of the scissors lets the reader see characters with innovative hairdos, a wide variety of clothing, and individualized physical features. The large heads balanced upon slender necks give the figures of the girls and boys a kind of fragility in a world that can be easily destabilized.

DILLON, LEO, AND DIANE DILLON. *Jazz on a Saturday Night.* Blue Sky Press/Scholastic, 2007. Gr. K–3*

Subdued shades and tints of brown, blue, and green with touches of yellow set the scene for an evening of jazz. Each page is a spirited invitation to enjoy the music of the historically great jazz personalities of another era. Dapper musicians dressed in cuff-linked shirts, with jacket and tie—and a few hats—join the fashionably dressed vocalist who will entertain an across-the-generations audience. The lights go up and Charlie Be-Bop Parker's golden saxophone responds to the notes from Miles Davis's trumpet. Skull-capped Thelonious Monk challenges the audience to respond to his unusual piano innovations. The audience seems enraptured as Ella Fitzgerald trickles her tongue around the rhythms of "scat" in a manner unequaled by any other.

With a subtle touch, this most creative art team diminishes shades of yellow in the spotlights, letting the audience in attendance know that the evening is over. The stage is empty. The musicians have gone. Jazz on a Saturday Night is a memory until the next time. Biographical sketches of the musicians appear in the endnotes.

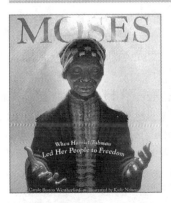

2007 WINNER

WEATHERFORD, CAROLE BOSTON.
Moses: When Harriet Tubman Led Her People to Freedom. Illustrated by Kadir Nelson.
Jump at the Sun/Hyperion Books for Children, 2006. Gr. K–3*

The account of the heroic slave who escaped and led three hundred of her people to freedom is well known. With an aura of deep spirituality, Nelson tells the story of Harriet Tubman's personal trials during her own escape. Dramatic paintings capture the pathos of the moment in dark shades of brown, blue, and deep green and then, with a masterstroke, keep an ever-present sign of hope and faith in the glow of yellow. In one scene, Tubman is wielding a huge ax, cutting into a huge tree stump. With the escapee on the move, we see in the dark of night the huge ax stuck, as if forever immobile, in that same tree stump—Tubman's determined end to servitude. We feel the pain, weariness, and loneliness as Harriet slumps against a darkened tree and bathes her feet in the cool creek water. Through it all, Nelson increases the symbolic color yellow, and at the end of her journey this light becomes like a radiant beam of praise as gnarled hands are raised in prayer and thanksgiving.

2007 HONORS

RAMPERSAD, ARNOLD, AND DAVID ROESSEL, EDS. *Langston Hughes. Poetry for Young People series.* Illustrated by Benny Andrews. Sterling, 2006. Gr. 7–10.

Andrews's spirited paintings illustrate twenty-six poems selected from the works of Langston Hughes. The combination of word and art portrays the African American experience with themes of hope, dreams of the future, the influence of music and dance, recollections of slavery and discrimination, and the resilience of the human spirit. Andrews's art, distinguished by elongated figures and minimal but effective use of detail, is painted mostly in varying shades of red, green, and blue. Providing an emotional as well as an aesthetic experience, this Coretta Scott King honor book will find a place in homes, schools, libraries, and the hearts of its readers.

MYERS, WALTER DEAN. *Jazz.* Illustrated by Christopher Myers. Holiday House, 2006. Gr. K–6.

It starts with the title page. With a flair of the dramatic, Christopher Myers immediately invites one to "hear" the music of the jazz era with, seemingly, a sound from the slender figures of a drummer. Pages filled with images then introduce the piano player, then the trumpet player whose full-blown cheeks blow out the notes. The rhythm of an unseen band has the Lindy Hoppers swinging across the double-page spread. The bass player, silhouetted against a blue background, captures the nostalgic sadness of Walter Dean Myers's blues poetry, "Waiting for me to come out to swing onto the empty avenue." *Jazz* has a harmonious blend of colors, skillfully constructed physical features, and a balanced representation of a variety of musicians. Through the effective combination of words and visuals, it can be shared as an important contribution to the history of music.

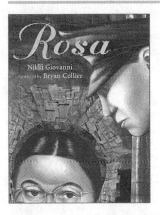

2006 WINNER

GIOVANNI, NIKKI. *Rosa.* Illustrated by Bryan Collier. Henry Holt, 2005. Gr. 3–5*

Noted for images featuring texture, pattern, and color that echo the complexities of the patchwork quilts created by African American artisans, Bryan Collier joins artists such as Romaire Bearden and Jacob Lawrence who have made the art of collage their very own.

The artist depicts Rosa Parks as a serene young seamstress in her work environment. Rosa's eyes shine out from behind glasses, welcoming the reader to join her on the journey to equality. Contrasting that image with the menacing hulk of the police hovering over her on the book's cover portends the drama that's soon to come.

Collier portrays Mrs. Parks's role as an exalted member of the human rights movement by including images of her with a golden halo. Collier creates a world that is timeless, yet anchored in 1955. Each visual, standing alone, has its own power. Collectively, the illustrations tell a story of Black resistance and determination and victory, through the life of one singular woman.

2006 HONOR

WILLIAMS, MARY. *Brothers in Hope: The Story of the Lost Boys of Sudan.* Illustrated by R. Gregory Christie. Lee & Low, 2005. Gr. 3–6.

Using acrylic paints, Christie captures the drama and trauma of thousands of young boys torn from their families in the horrific raids on the villages of Sudan. The scenes come to life, showing a multitude of scantily clothed, cocoa-colored young boys making a fear-filled trek into unknown territory. A swirling swatch of green depicts the wide river that the boys must cross if they are to reach safety. Touches of paint become bobbing heads as one by one the band of "brothers" emerge on the shore, with no loss of life. Christie focuses on education as the key to survival, first through the picture of young boys struggling to replace play with attention to schoolbooks, and later through the image of a lone young man reading a book, preparing for the future. The main character in *Brothers in Hope* is in reality Valentino Deng, now studying international law. As in previous books, Christie's characters have oversized heads. When asked why he depicts them that way, Christie responded quietly and philosophically: "That is where the mind is."

2005 WINNER

SHANGE, NTOZAKE. *Ellington Was Not a Street.* **Illustrated by Kadir Nelson.** Simon & Schuster Books for Young Readers, 2004. Gr. 3–5.

Today, Ellington is a tiny street in lower Manhattan, but the street Nelson shows us is one where the movers and shakers of the mid-1920s and 1930s met to discuss important social matters. The "young miss" of the house welcomes the towering Paul Robeson into the parlor. Robeson joins in serious conversation with W. E. B. Du Bois. Many musicians are among those who cross the threshold. Nelson gives each character a distinctive identity. In one house on Ellington Street, neatly dressed gentlemen discuss the affairs of the day while enjoying a game of cards, spied on by the "young miss." With all the comings and goings, there is still a constant sense of family.

Along with the realistic personal portrayals, Nelson's background scenes give evidence of careful study of the period; flowered wallpaper in the parlor, the huge grandfather clock in the spacious hallway, oversized furniture, and then the tiny lace doily on the coffee table. For a look back in time and an introduction to influential personalities of an earlier generation, *Ellington Was Not a Street* extends the author's recollections in lyrical verse.

2005 HONORS

HAMILTON, VIRGINIA. *The People Could Fly: The Picture Book.* Illustrated by Leo Dillon and Diane Dillon. Knopf, 2004. Gr. K–5.

Somber black endpapers with a feeling of embossed feathers forecast the sorrow-filled legend told in the Dillons's dramatic illustrations for *The People Could Fly.* The picture book is a new interpretation in which some who are dragged into captivity happen to have wings. With creative use of muted earth colors, the symbiotic Dillon palette captures the agony, fear, and helplessness of those chained in a ship's hold. The illustrations of a mother's anguish and a child's pain at the whip-swinging overseer's cruelty reflect their desperation. The placement of hands speaks volumes as an ancient bearded "spirit of freedom" appears, knowing the time has come to set wings in motion. Like a graceful dancer, the first flier leaps toward the heavens. Others, suddenly adorned in clothing of geometric splendor, begin the flight to freedom.

On the closing page, the Dillons pay a final tribute to their dear friend Virginia Hamilton, as she joins the assembly of the people who, with wings unfurled, could fly. One look is not enough to absorb all the stories, all the emotions, and all the mystic history that the Dillons have embodied in this picture-book version.

HOLIDAY, BILLIE, AND ARTHUR HERZOG JR. *God Bless the Child.* Illustrated by Jerry Pinkney. Amistad/HarperCollins, 2004. Gr. 2–6.

Pinkney's visual interpretation of Billie Holiday's vocal commemoration of the Great Migration of the 1930s looks closely at the toil-worn faces of Negroes toiling endlessly in southern cotton fields. Deft use of line and color captures the range of moods of family members as one group heads north. A turn of the page and we find a startling contrast with scenes of hustle and bustle in the city—El trains, automobiles, tall buildings, and busy factories.

Contrasting shades and tints of the same color in the clothing, and posturing in body positions, bespeak a subtle snobbery between the ones who have "made it" in the city and the new arrivals. The closing scene is a wordless message that education is the key for each one who would "have his own." From a study of history to his own creative artistry, a master storyteller with brush and paint has given visual life to the meaning of *God Bless the Child.* (The accompanying CD is a reproduction of Billie Holiday singing this plaintive song.)

2005 JOHN STEPTOE NEW TALENT AWARD

ROBERTS, BRENDA C. *Jazzy Miz Mozetta.* **Illustrated by Frank Morrison.**
Farrar, Straus and Giroux, 2004. Gr. Pre-K–3.

In a neomannerist style, Morrison portrays an African American ethnic community full of life and joyous energy. His story of an evening of dance and friendship employs color and movement to create a warm, close relationship between readers and characters in the book, who come alive through the artist's use of physical and emotional expression, body posture, and color. The movement of the dance can be experienced by all.

As Miz Mozetta, in her fancy dress and special blue dancing shoes, ventures out into the evening, vibrant colors heighten the excitement, and almost exaggerated shapes express life in action among intergenerational members of the community. We can feel the tension when Miz Mozetta turns her back, if only momentarily, on those who rejected her and the understanding when Miz Mozetta and the others realize that their community isn't complete without the youth. It's a joyous closing when young and old join in a breathless jitterbug fling. Morrison's perceptive interpretation of Roberts's story of what it means to be a community deservedly earned him a Coretta Scott King Book Award for new talent.

2004 WINNER

BRYAN, ASHLEY. *Beautiful Blackbird.* Atheneum, 2003. Gr. K–2.

From the Ila-speaking people of Zambia, *Beautiful Blackbird* achieves excellence in children's literature through both the illustrative and the textual artistry of its creator. Bryan's ability to capture the rhythm and cadence of the African folk tradition is unparalleled. From endpaper to endpaper, Bryan's cut-paper figures fill the pages with strong imagery. The collage technique, combining the powerful blackness of the central character with the brilliant contrasting colors of the birds, all set against stark white pages, makes this memorable story a visual treat.

Bryan has perfected the language of movement in this retelling of how each in a merry throng of birds comes to sport a bit of black in his plumage. *Beautiful Blackbird* carries a strong message of pride and self-confidence, attesting to the fact that black is beautiful. When Ringdove begs for a bit of color, Blackbird admonishes, "Color on the outside is not what's on the inside. . . . I'll be me and you'll be you." A delightful selection for reading aloud or for looking at over and over.

2004 HONORS

NELSON, VAUNDA MICHEAUX. *Almost to Freedom.* Illustrated by Colin Bootman. Carolrhoda, 2003. Gr. 1–3.

Painted against a stark background, each scene in this poignant story interprets a part of the author's historically based telling of the African American slave's constant quest for freedom. The narrator is a tiny homemade doll who, through Bootman's use of brush and palette, emanates an aura of response and interaction. As the drama unfolds, the visuals capture the many moods surrounding the events in the escape attempt. The use of muted colors in the clothing of each character, coupled with the carefully designed body positions of each, sustains the tension of the story from its very beginning. Then, in keeping with the comforting surprise ending of the story, the artist clothes the newest owner of the homemade doll in a dress of brilliant sunshine yellow.

NOLEN, JERDINE. *Thunder Rose.* Illustrated by Kadir Nelson. Whistle/Harcourt, 2003. Gr. K–3.

Jerdine Nolen wrote this original tall tale to celebrate African Americans who settled the American West. Kadir Nelson's illustrations capture the joy and the power of its young heroine. Using oil, watercolor, and pencil, Nelson depicts the storm that greets Rose's birth, the literally electrifying moment when the newborn girl grabs hold of a lightning bolt, and the family's love and wonder in the presence of their extraordinary child. Shades of brown and blue convey the closeness of Thunder Rose's family and the endless western skies under which they live. Nelson is especially successful in creating expressive characters. Readers will laugh at a startled cow being suckled by the infant girl and sense Rose's strength as she wrestles the steer to the ground. Whether Rose is surveying the parched land or taming a tornado, Nelson's illustrations depict a spunky, endearing child with larger-than-life powers.

2004 JOHN STEPTOE NEW TALENT AWARD

COX, JUDY. *My Family Plays Music.* **Illustrated by Elbrite Brown.** Holiday House, 2003. Gr. Pre-K–3.

Clang the cymbals, tap the triangle, ring the handbell, shake the tambourine, dance in the street! Executed with brilliantly colored cut-paper figures, the artwork of this book invites one and all to celebrate the joys of music that ranges from classical string quartets to bluegrass to modern jazz and much more.

Brown's illustrations capture the exuberance of a multiethnic group of people sharing the joy and universality of harmonious sound. The creatively prolific use of rounded lines depicting characters and instruments, set against an uncluttered background, extends this merry tale. The simplicity of the instruments played by the always identifiable protagonist with her well-tended cornrow braids is an invitation for readers to make their own music. Colorful mini reproductions of the music scenes add visual interest to the book's informative glossary. This book is a visual treat that sings and dances from cover to cover.

2003 WINNER

GRIMES, NIKKI. *Talkin' About Bessie: The Story of Aviator Elizabeth Coleman.* **Illustrated by E. B. Lewis.** Orchard, 2002. Gr. 2–5*

E. B. Lewis's watercolors illustrate Nikki Grimes's poetic prose and free verse to portray the life of the first female pilot of African American descent and one of America's most daring barnstormers. The format chosen has Coleman's friends and relatives gathered at Bessie's death to reminisce about her life. For each speaker, Lewis has painted a small sepia portrait and a full-page representation of the speaker's recollections. His water-saturated colors and limited palette—predominantly browns, blues, and greens—hint at the photographs of an earlier time. As the mourners gather, Bessie watches, smiling from a photograph on the mantel. By placing a mirror behind the photograph, Lewis makes room for the reader to join the gathering. Expressive compositions and careful choice of details contribute to the narrative power of the illustrations. In one scene, Bessie hangs laundry on the line, but large and in the foreground are jars in which she is saving precious coins for her education. In another scene, a bigoted white woman recalls Bessie's assertiveness. Lewis shows Bessie and the woman holding tight to a laundry basket. The tension in their grip is a mark of Bessie's strength and determination. From the close-up portrait of Bessie on the cover to the soaring plane in the book's final scene, Lewis's illustrations convey the struggles and triumphs of Bessie Coleman's life. The authenticity of clothing, artifacts, and settings are based on Lewis's careful research of the period in which Coleman lived (1896–1926).

2003 HONORS

PERDOMO, WILLIE. *Visiting Langston.* **Illustrated by Bryan Collier.** Henry Holt, 2002. Gr. 2–4*

Visiting Langston takes Collier to the streets of his Harlem neighborhood to celebrate the centennial of Renaissance poet Langston Hughes's birth. A smiling young girl, her writing journal held close to her heart, goes with her father to visit the house where Hughes wrote "poems like jazz," "sang like love," and "cried like blues." The artist's signature watercolors and cut-paper collage provide texture and detail for Perdomo's poetic text. As the words sing of "what Africa means to me," our young girl gazes out her window at a sky that takes on the shape of that continent. The creative inclusion of an old-fashioned typewriter, the use of a technique that gives texture to the brownstone stoop, the painting of airy green leaves, and the use of fabric patterns blend seamlessly to give visibility to a now gone time. The positioning of father and daughter in each scene, like an ode to love, speaks convincingly of the warm relationship they share as together they experience the pride and joy of a young African American girl's visit to the home of her literary hero.

DILLON, LEO, AND DIANE DILLON. *Rap a Tap Tap: Here's Bojangles—Think of That!* Blue Sky Press/Scholastic, 2002. Gr. Pre-K–2.

Rap a Tap Tap is the delicious sound tapped out by Mr. Bill "Bojangles" Robinson for city children, park-sitting parents, folk making a living through small businesses, people waiting at soup kitchens, and dressed-up ladies and gentlemen.

As Bill "Bojangles" dances through the pages, readers get a view of city life—the overhead trains, street vendors' vegetable carts, high rises, and even rainy-day parades.

Robinson is not dancing alone. In the background of each scene, a colorfully dressed ethnic mix of joyous people of all ages swings to the moves of this high-stepping dancer. With their impeccable skill, Leo and Diane Dillon have seamlessly woven into this story biographical matter and social commentary.

Set in Robinson's hometown, Harlem, *Rap a Tap Tap* is a creative introduction to the art of a talented performer and a handsome book for readers of all ages.

2003 JOHN STEPTOE NEW TALENT AWARD

DUBURKE, RANDY. *The Moon Ring.* Chronicle, 2002. Gr. K–2.

Randy DuBurke tells the story of Maxine, a young girl who feels the magic in the air as she sits on the porch with her grandmother on a hot summer night. It is the night of the blue moon, the second full moon in that month. Maxine's magical trip begins when she finds a silver ring the size of a stove burner ring. When she wishes for cooler weather, she is suddenly transported to the Antarctic. Just as quickly she finds herself riding a giraffe across the African savanna. When a pride of lions confronts them, Maxine wishes she was far away in New York City—and there she is—atop the Empire State Building. The romp continues until Maxine is back home telling her family about her adventures. The family decides it was either a dream or the product of a great imagination—that is, all except Grandma, who saw the seal, the penguin, and the giraffe outside the kitchen window.

DuBurke's cartoonlike illustrations fill each page with exaggerated shapes and expressions. Maxine's athleticism and joy-filled expressions are evident in her once-in-a-lifetime blue moon adventure.

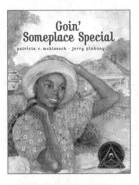

2002 WINNER

MCKISSACK, PATRICIA C. *Goin' Someplace Special.* Illustrated by Jerry Pinkney. Atheneum, 2001. Gr. K–5.

With watercolor over pencil illustrations, Jerry Pinkney brings warmth, movement, and vivid color to this story of a young girl on her first trip alone in the segregated southern town of Nashville. The use of clothing, hairstyles, and automobile details, contribute to the authenticity of the 1950s setting. Rich colors for 'Tricia Ann contrast with the paler, more neutral shades used for people and the places around her. Full page spreads work well with text and provide a sense of movement on the journey. The expressive faces of the characters during their conversations break the isolation that the Jim Crow laws attempt to impose. Pinkney uses composition and art to accentuate the strength, courage, and perseverance described in the text. The yellow light glowing in the culminating scene highlighting the Nashville Public Library emphasizes the warmth of success and freedom achieved.

2002 HONOR

RAPPAPORT, DOREEN. *Martin's Big Words: The Life of Dr. Martin Luther King, Jr.* Illustrated by Bryan Collier. Jump at the Sun/Hyperion Books for Children, 2001. Gr. K–2*

Designed for young readers, Rappaport's brief, skillfully woven, carefully selected quotations present defining moments in Dr. King's life. Collier's watercolors and collage enhance the drama, devotion, and dedication of the man and his mission. A Civil War flag hangs high as a young Martin points to the "whites only" drinking fountain. The American flag is front and center as two freedom marchers hold hands and Dr. King speaks during the March on Washington. Light shining through a stained-glass panel illuminates Dr. King's face as he preaches. The lighting of the candle symbolizes a hope that the world will discover a way to live together. Collier's work reflects his attention to all details of design and his strong feeling for his subject.

2002 JOHN STEPTOE NEW TALENT AWARD

WILES, DEBORAH. *Freedom Summer.* Illustrated by Jerome Lagarrigue. Simon & Schuster, 2001. Gr. K–3.

An innovative use of color marks Jerome Lagarrigue's illustrations in this story based on the author's experience. The heat of the underlying golds, greens, and browns is reminiscent of a hot summer day. The cool shades of purple, pink, and blue add depth that matches the strong feeling evoked by the story of an integrated friendship in a segregated community. Joe and John Henry have shared summers together their whole lives but have had to adapt to stringent rules that govern the options for John Henry—just because of his color. At last, the courts have ruled that everything must be integrated. Emotional ups and downs are mirrored in the paintings' colors as well as in the expressions on the two boys' faces. Adults are mostly background figures, vague and somewhat blurry. The focus is on the boys. The illustrator captures with dramatic accuracy the way these young people cope with injustice. The resolution is as discomforting as it is realistic, but Lagarrigue's vibrant illustrations bring warmth and tenderness to the main characters without falsifying history.

2001 WINNER

COLLIER, BRYAN. *Uptown.* Henry Holt, 2000. Gr. K–3.

On the title page, a confident young man stands poised to give readers a personal tour of the streets of Harlem. Collier, who lives and works in that community, uses watercolors and cut-page collage in vibrant colors and intriguing patterns to illustrate his own brief but lively text. In changing scenes, historic brownstone houses are fashioned from chocolate bars, shoppers wear richly textured African fabrics, Van DerZee photographs are displayed on building walls, and young girls in Sunday finery walk to church. The sounds of jazz and the Boys Choir of Harlem fill "Harlem . . . Harlem is my World." The reds, yellows, greens, and blues used to letter the title and text cheerfully complement the multileveled but very accessible design.

Young readers will respond to this proud and loving tribute that portrays a community alive with music, food, faith, and art.

2001 HONORS

ROCKWELL, ANNE. *Only Passing Through: The Story of Sojourner Truth.* Illustrated by R. Gregory Christie. Random House, 2000. Gr. 3–5*

Distinctively Negroid features, rendered with respect and sensitivity, distinguish the African American characters in this young readers' edition of the life of Sojourner Truth. When viewing Christie's illustrations, the first thing one notices is the emphasis on the characters' heads, heads that are large, atop elongated bodies. When asked about this particular trait, the illustrator's quiet reply was, "I focus on the head because that is where the mind is." Close study of the facial expressions of the slave owners and those they would keep in bondage reveals a solid contrast of evil versus good. Somber tones of brown, black, and terra-cotta dominate the pages as one traces Sojourner Truth's heroic journey from slavery to freedom.

RAPPAPORT, DOREEN. *Freedom River.* Illustrated by Bryan Collier. Jump at the Sun/Hyperion Books for Children, 2000. Gr. 3–5*

Based on a true event, *Freedom River* is the inspiring story of John Parker, one of the conductors on the Underground Railroad. He leads a family to freedom across the Ohio River from Kentucky to Ohio. Parker, born a slave, after buying his freedom, repeatedly risks his life to help others. For one journey, he must sneak into the slaveholder's bedroom, where Isaac and Sarah's baby slept at night. This arrangement was planned to thwart the parents' desire to flee. The escape, though filled with danger, is successful. Rappaport's text conveys a sense of intense anxiety. Collier uses cut-paper collage and watercolors as perfect accompaniments to the mood. Intense shades of purple and blue are used in the nighttime scenes. The endpapers show a map of the route along the Ohio River. A special feature of the book's design can be seen in the portraits of the ancestors who provided spiritual guidance to African Americans. Collier used the leaders of his church as models and adorned their photographs with wavy lines representing the undulating motion of the river to freedom.

HOWARD, ELIZABETH. *Virgie Goes to School with Us Boys.* Illustrated by
E. B. Lewis. Simon & Schuster, 2000. Gr. K–2.

Lewis's expressive full-page watercolors capture the greens and browns of
the rural setting for this true story of a family's quest for education and its
availability at the Quaker-run Warner Institute in Jonesborough, Tennessee.

The illustrator masterfully contrasts the starkness of the family's living
conditions in their drab brown cabin with the brightening hues on the
clothing of both the boys and Virgie as they take the long walk to school.
One cannot miss the slight touch of humor as a mud-splattered Virgie
smiles after falling into a creek that lies along the way. The seemingly limit-
less length of dark trees and the road that has neither beginning nor end
evoke the distance the young people must travel in their quest for an education. To suggest the time period, Lewis uses special touches of paint to illustrate the quill pen, the slate, and the rough-hewn desk and benches. In the
final picture, Virgie's sparkling eyes and infectious smile perfectly capture
the book's theme, the joy of "learning—to be free."

2000 WINNER

SIEGELSON, KIM. *In the Time of the Drums.*
Illustrated by Brian Pinkney. Jump at the Sun/
Hyperion Books for Children, 1999. Gr. 3–5.

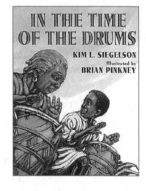

"In the long ago time before now on an island fringed
by marsh meadows and washed by ocean tides, men
and women and their children lived enslaved." Thus
begins Kim Siegelson's story inspired by Gullah
oral traditions. It is the story of Twi, her grandson
Mentu, and her magical escape from bondage. The harmonious colors of the
illustrations depict the heat of the sun, the cool of the water, and the brown
earth that the enslaved "worked from dark of morning to dark of night, har-
vesting what they could not keep." As Mentu drummed with Twi until the
rhythms felt as natural to him as his own heart beating, "the bronze color
of the drums complement the beautiful bronze shades of their bodies." Near
the books end, Pinkney illustrates a calm sunset scene with Mentu watching a flock of birds. The rising birds suggest the spirits of the slaves now free

from bondage. The scene is an evocative prelude to the lively closing illustration in which a contemporary boy and girl play skin drums as Mentu taught his children "and they taught their own children . . . through slave time and freedom time and on up until now time."

2000 HONORS

MOLLEL, TOLOLWA. *My Rows and Piles of Coins.* Illustrated by E. B. Lewis. Clarion, 1999. Gr. K–2.

Nineteen sixties Tanzania is the setting for this story based on events in the author's childhood. Young Saruni helps his mother at the market, and on this particular day she gives him ten-cent coins to buy something for himself. He decides to save the money to buy a bicycle so that he can help his mother carry her products to market. Saruni learns to ride a bicycle and finally, with help and understanding, he gets the transportation he needs to help his mother. Saruni next dreams of saving enough money to buy a cart to pull behind the bicycle to further lighten his mother's load.

E. B. Lewis's expressive, watercolor illustrations re-create the bustling activity of the Tanzanian marketplace. The pictures capture the hopes and feelings of the young boy as he works with his mother and practices riding a bike. As Saruni walks through the marketplace, his mother and father watch their son with protective concern at his final triumph of riding the bike purchased with his "rows and piles of coins."

MYERS, CHRISTOPHER. *Black Cat.* Scholastic, 1999. Gr. 3–6.

There is an unmistakable sense of independence in the way the sleek Black Cat walks the streets of Harlem, balancing faultlessly past empty bottles on an old brick wall or in quest of a mouse meal, challenging a subway as it races through its dark tunnel. Myers's innovative use of acrylics, collage, and photography invites readers to view Harlem from Black Cat's perspective, moving gracefully through the blur of rushing traffic or defying gravity while walking along the roof edges of dimly lit tenement houses. Myers captures the changing shapes of the cat as it squeezes through the crisscrosses of a fence to leap effortlessly through the bright orange basketball rim on a deserted court. At the close of the day, signaled by the changing blues of the evening sky, Black Cat, with defiant, fiery yellow eyes, seems to respond to the reader's question, "We want to know where's your home?" Black Cat answers, "Anywhere I roam."

The stalwart Black Cat's city journey is a masterful blend of poetry and picture.

1999 WINNER

IGUS, TOYOMI. *I See the Rhythm.* **Illustrated by Michele Wood.** Children's Book Press, 1998. Gr. 3–5.

I See the Rhythm is a multilayered history of African American music that celebrates the far-reaching impact of this art form. The rich text includes words from songs of various eras, definitions of musical styles, and valuable chronological time lines. Vibrant, energetic, expressionistic paintings, blended with innovative fonts and creative page design, enrich this visual chronicle of African American music from the drumbeats of Africa to stirring gospel to the contemporary rhythms of funk, rap, and hip-hop.

Wood's paintings mix a variety of styles and vivid colors to suggest musical style and tone. The illustrator has also incorporated much historical detail in her paintings, making them rich explorations of the text. The choice of colors and the variety in layout make this volume a feast for the eyes and drive home in a most dramatic fashion the importance, the depth, and the vitality of the musical forms that the work encompasses.

1999 HONORS

THOMAS, JOYCE CAROL. *I Have Heard of a Land.* **Illustrated by Floyd Cooper.** HarperCollins, 1998. Gr. 3–6*

Lush paintings on double-page spreads heighten the sense of place in this depiction of the historic land runs of the late 1800s. It was a time when Black pioneer settlers were offered the freedom of land ownership in the Oklahoma Territory. The book especially honors the female participants who "dared to act on their dreams." This artistic rendering presents the vastness of the Oklahoma Territory and reflects the strength and determination of the African American pioneers.

The skillful use of light and color evokes a vivid picture of the character of the land. The rich earth tones perfectly fit the descriptions in the text. Artist Cooper is most successful in depicting the contrast between the great expanse of land and the individuals who sought to tame it as well as the connectedness between the land and those same individuals. With studied but not overworked detail, Cooper captures the challenge and spirit in the faces of the settlers he portrays. This illustrated history will bring to life for young readers a little-known aspect of African American history.

CURTIS, GAVIN. *The Bat Boy and His Violin.* Illustrated by E. B. Lewis. Simon & Schuster, 1998. Gr. 3–5.

Evocative watercolor paintings illuminate this warm family story set in the late 1940s. Music lover Reginald wants to practice his violin, but his dad, the manager of the Dukes of the Negro National League, needs a batboy. Despite the fact that Reginald is preparing for an upcoming concert, his dad insists that he accompany the team. However, Reginald finds a way while traveling with the team to pursue his first love—music—and at the same time lift the morale of the players.

E. B. Lewis's graceful watercolor paintings bring a special dimension to this unique story of intergenerational male bonding. The artist skillfully uses this technique to portray the time, the place, and the mood of the story. His careful attention to detail provides an authenticity that makes this book worthy of special attention. The almost delicate watercolor paintings provide an interesting backdrop to the masculinity of the baseball scenes and imply the gentle and sensitive nature of the men despite the physical nature of their game.

PINKNEY, ANDREA DAVIS. *Duke Ellington: The Piano Prince and His Orchestra.* Illustrated by Brian Pinkney. Hyperion Books for Children, 1998. Gr. 3–5*

Andrea Davis Pinkney's rhythmic text and artist Brian Pinkney's vibrant illustrations trace Duke Ellington's career from his childhood as a reluctant piano student to his triumphant success as a composer and orchestra leader. The swirling patterns and pulsing colors of Brian Pinkney's illustrations capture the dynamism of Duke Ellington's music. The artist uses scratch-board renderings with dyes, gouache, and paint to make the text come alive. At times, the visuals are larger than life. The creative placement of figures on each page informs the reader of the important role that music played in Ellington's life. With the passage of time, Ellington's musical influence grew and expanded, and the artist shows this to the reader while the author explains it in the text.

Pinkney's use of line and color brings a vibrancy to the text that reflects the many moods of Ellington's music. His use of visuals and space, from the music exploding from the instruments right up to the A train seemingly riding off the page, will engage not only young readers but also music lovers of all ages.

1999 JOHN STEPTOE NEW TALENT AWARD

CHOCOLATE, DEBBI. *The Piano Man.* **Illustrated by Eric Velasquez.** Walker, 1998. Gr. K–2.

In this intergenerational story, a young girl tells, with great affection, the story of her grandfather, a musician who played the piano for many years. His love for music carried him from silent movies to vaudeville and finally to legitimate theater. When opportunities for performing were no longer available, he tuned pianos for a living, always passing on his love for music from era to era to his daughter and granddaughter.

Eric Velasquez's spirited paintings engage the reader and add life to the story. His clever illustrations begin with the closed curtain on the endpaper of the front cover and move to an open curtain on the title page. The animation in the faces transmits the exuberance the characters feel. Color choice is strong, and the effective use of light balances the many warm shades of brown.

1998 WINNER

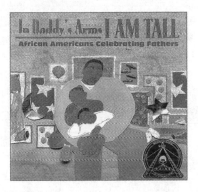

STEPTOE, JAVAKA. *In Daddy's Arms I Am Tall: African Americans Celebrating Fathers.* Lee & Low, 1997. Gr. K–2.

With imagination and creativity, Javaka Steptoe designed the illustrations in this eye-intriguing volume to complement poems by several poets writing in praise of fathers and fatherhood. The designs are developed from such three-dimensional objects as buttons, chalk, pieces of window screen, paper collages, and other materials, thus giving exciting life and color to the selected poems. Steptoe discusses the variety of images:

> Each of the poems was so different, and I wanted each to have its own individuality. And so each illustration invites you to take a second look, less some innovative detail be missed.

When speaking of the art in *In Daddy's Arms I Am Tall,* Steptoe says:

> I've thought about illustrating children's books all my life . . . [then] I was thinking a lot about my relationships with my father and ideas of manhood. I thought this would be the perfect book.

The four years that it took to complete this book attest to the seriousness with which Javaka Steptoe reflected on his relationship with his father, the late, great illustrator John Steptoe.

1998 HONORS

BRYAN, ASHLEY. *Ashley Bryan's ABC of African American Poetry.* Atheneum, 1997. Gr. K–5.

Vivid tempera paintings, replete with significant symbolic information, grace the pages of this oversized volume. With care and focus, Bryan has selected the works of twenty-five African and African American poets and one ever popular spiritual to introduce the youth of all cultures to the strength and beauty of these writers' words. The moods vary from poignant to humorous to unforgettably thought provoking. In a masterful blend of sound and symbols, one sees and hears the breaking of the chains as

Robert Hayden tells of Sojourner Truth walking barefoot out of slavery or God's laughter in Samuel Hayden's tribute in "Satch." Blazing firmaments, strength-filled dark eyes, love-filled brown faces of family, and the eloquent portrayal of the sturdy though time-worn face in Margaret Walker's tribute to grandmothers are just a few of the elements that showed the Coretta Scott King awards jury that this was an unforgettable collection worthy to be honored.

DIAKITÉ, BABA WAGUÉ. *The Hunterman and the Crocodile: A West African Folktale.* Scholastic, 1997. Gr. 3–5.

Bamba the crocodile and his family are on a pilgrimage to Mecca when they run out of food and water and plead with Donso the Hunterman to help them return home. After reluctantly agreeing, Donso is betrayed by Bamba, who threatens to eat him. From this beginning, the reader is led into a tale of treachery—a reminder of humankind's selfish use of plants and animals. The tale underscores the importance of learning to live together in harmony.

Baba Wagué Diakité has illustrated the storytelling with stylized, hand-painted tiles whose folkloric quality complement the text. Black figures cavort on a background of muted earth tones with subtle touches of color. The striking design of the book is evident in its interplay of decorative and representational elements, its rhythmic patterns, and its dynamic use of line. All of these features do much to extend this telling of a traditional tale. Although the author/illustrator's work reflects his West African background, his playful illustrations are an expression of a unique artistic talent that reaches beyond all geographic boundaries.

MYERS, WALTER DEAN. *Harlem.* Illustrated by Christopher Myers. Scholastic, 1997. Gr. 6–8.

The community of Harlem has for decades served as a touchstone for numerous writers and visual artists. This father-and-son collaboration adds to that rich body of work. Christopher Myers portrays street scenes, rooftops, a church interior, the A train subway, fire escapes, nightclubs, a basketball court, living rooms, and individual people in single- and double-page spreads. His collages incorporate singular moments—hair braiding, hoop shooting, funerals, and neighbors chatting—vignettes of life in this vitality-filled community. Myers's mixed-media works illuminate the poetic history of the past and the present glories of Harlem's people, their music, and their art and literature, and provide a visual counterpoint to the lyrical poetry of his father. The original artwork from this oversized dynamic picture book of cultural history has been exhibited at the Studio Museum of Harlem on 125th Street.

1997 WINNER

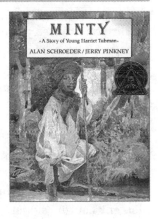

SCHROEDER, ALAN. *Minty: A Story of Young Harriet Tubman.* Illustrated by Jerry Pinkney. Dial, 1996. Gr. K–2.

Alan Schroeder's fictionalized account of young Harriet Tubman, who refused to be the "docile slave," provides the setting for Jerry Pinkney's dramatic visual interpretation of the vitality, determination, and ingenuity that marked this remarkable heroine's life. Careful research enabled this serious illustrator to depict authentic details about the dress, food, and living conditions of the plantation slaves. His own sensitivity, historical background, and passionate concern allowed Pinkney to portray in moving scenes the strength, courage, fears, and dangers young Harriet faced with unmitigated courage. Detailed watercolor spreads coupled with a master illustrator's use of space, color, and perspective provide scenes of cabin life, threatening forests, and the wild-eyed fear of the would-be runaway. The artistic attention given to all aspects of the story enrich this narration that introduces young readers to an unforgettable personality later known as the Moses of her people.

1997 HONORS

ADEDJOUMA, DAVIDA, ED. *The Palm of My Heart: Poetry by African American Children.* Illustrated by R. Gregory Christie. Lee & Low, 1996. Gr. K–3.

African American young people who are a part of the Inner City Youth League wrote the stirring, pride-filled words that inspired Gregory Christie's illustrations in this very special collaboration. The artist's paintings capture the joy and exultation with which the young writers see their future.

His depiction of a young lady on stilts raises a proud Black girl to unknown heights even as she proclaims that "Black is me—Tall, dark and wonderful." In some scenes, there is a sense of spirituality, such as in the image of a church that looks down protectively on a close-knit gathering. The writers honor the elders, and Christie's art gives visual reality to the honor in a simple cross-generational painting that says, indeed, that "Black power is . . . long life."

Christie's muted paintings, like a musical accompaniment, support and interpret but never overpower the lyrical writings of the young poets.

LAUTURE, DENIZÉ. *Running the Road to ABC.* Illustrated by Reynold Ruffins. Simon & Schuster, 1996. Gr. K–3.

Sparkling with life in both text and illustration, *Running the Road to ABC* reflects a joy of learning. The story, set in Haiti, tells of six children who rise before dawn and run through the beautiful countryside on their way to school. Ruffins's magnificent, brightly colored gouache illustrations complement Lauture's poetic text. His images capture many stories of the culture—a breakfast of cornmeal, yams, and perhaps some Congo beans; book bags made from palm leaves; and the simple, open-windowed schoolroom.

The pictures give one a sense of place as the illustrator uses the bright colors of the Caribbean to great effect. There is visual poetry as the paintings show first dawn in the village, stars still twinkling in the sky, the rooster sleeping while a mother bids her son goodbye on his way to ABC. From this beginning to the double-page illustration of the eager children watching attentively, paper and pencil in hand, this book sings with joy in words and pictures. Ruffins's paintings, filled with flora and fauna, frogs, snails, lizards, butterflies, donkeys, and gorgeously plumed birds, transport the reader to this tropic land.

ENGLISH, KAREN. *Neeny Coming, Neeny Going.* Illustrated by Synthia Saint James. BridgeWater, 1996. Gr. K–3.

Karen English takes readers back to the 1950s, a time of change when residents of the Daufuskie Island left their homes to seek another way of life on the mainland. Young Essie awaits the return of her cousin Neeny, who was one who had left the island. Synthia Saint James has captured the bittersweet mood of Essie's excitement at the thought of Neeny's return, and the emptiness she feels because she realizes that Neeny, although physically there, has not really come back.

Flat, collage-like illustrations portray life on the island: bogging for crabs, weaving baskets from sweetgrass, and picking blackberries. Simple features and bright shapes show Essie running excitedly through the island to tell of Neeny's return. With this same simplicity, Saint James illustrates the fading joy and the indignation and sadness as Neeny says goodbye. Readers will find particular significance in the memory quilt Essie gives Neeny on Neeny's departure. Words and pictures in *Neeny Coming, Neeny Going* convey to the reader a culturally specific place and a part of the African American experience that has a sense of universality.

1996 WINNER

FEELINGS, TOM. *The Middle Passage:* White Ships/Black Cargo. Dial, 1995. Gr. 9–12*

Feelings created a series of illustrations that eloquently describe the capture of slaves in Africa and their horrendous trip across the Atlantic to America. *The Middle Passage* opens with a sun-filled African landscape. In successive images, Feelings depicts the forced march of captured slaves, the violence and claustrophobia of slave ships, and the desperate and futile attempts to escape the ships by diving into the shark-infested waters. Powerful bodies of Black slaves stand out against the ghostly forms of their white tormentors. Swirling shapes echo howls of despair and yearnings for freedom.

In the introduction, Feelings writes that it was while he was living in Ghana that his "drawings became more fluid and flowing. Rhythmic lines of motion, like a drumbeat, started to appear in my work, and a style that incorporated a dance consciousness surfaced."

In completing *The Middle Passage*, Feelings expressed the hope that "those chains of the past, those shackles that physically bound us together against our wills could, in the telling, become spiritual links that willingly bind us together now and into the future."

1996 HONORS

HAMILTON, VIRGINIA. *Her Stories: African American Folktales, Fairy Tales, and True Tales.* Illustrated by Leo Dillon and Diane Dillon. Scholastic, 1995. Gr. 5–8.

The paintings that illustrate *Her Stories* capture the mood of each female-oriented tale, with meticulous attention shown to the details needed to give visual vitality to this superb collection. One cannot miss the crafty eyes in the diminutive rabbit in "Little Girl and Buh Rabby." The mermaid with stringy, vine-like hair does indeed float in a jar of green water. Note how menacing the eerie, cold-green, chiseled-tooth, wart-faced hag is that rides Marie's back in "Marie and the Boo Hag." By contrast, there is the quiet dignity of reality in the portraits of the women in the biographical section. The reader's eye will respond to the art of the award-winning Dillons, even as the ear responds to the words of Her Stories.

SAN SOUCI, ROBERT. *The Faithful Friend.* Illustrated by Brian Pinkney. Simon & Schuster, 1995. Gr. K–4.

Set on the island of Martinique, Robert San Souci's story of two faithful friends, one white and one Black, is replete with elements of the area's culture: magic, zombies, dark forces, and romance. Brian Pinkney's specialized scratchboard technique, enriched with touches of oil-paint colors, captures the changing moods of the story. Dramatic moments from the narrative come to life when the artist shows the faithful Hippolyte slowly turned to stone through the magic of the zombies. The zombies are formidable figures in their dark clothing, weaving their spells in the gloom of the tropical landscape. In contrast, the illustrator shows the delicate texture of the young bride's dress at her marriage to Clement. One can almost feel the material of the clothing of other characters. Through the drawings of the furnishings in the home, scenery in the lush tropical landscape, and small details of facial expressions and body language, the illustrator displays his skill in putting into visual perspective the words of the story.

ILLUSTRATIONS FROM
AWARD-WINNING BOOKS

2005 WINNER

Ellington Was Not a Street, **KADIR NELSON**

Illustration © 2004 by Kadir Nelson from *Ellington Was Not a Street* written by Ntozake Shange.
Published by Simon & Schuster Books for Young Readers, an imprint of Simon & Schuster
Children's Publishing. Used with permission of the publisher.

1974 WINNER

Ray Charles, **GEORGE FORD**

Illustrations © 1974 by George Ford. Permission arranged
with Lee & Low Books Inc., New York, NY 10016.

1991 WINNER

Aïda, **LEO DILLON AND DIANE DILLON**

From *Aïda* by Leontyne Price. Illustration © 1990 by Leo Dillon and Diane Dillon.
Reprinted by permission of Houghton Mifflin Harcourt Publishing Company. All rights reserved.

2006 WINNER

Rosa, **BRYAN COLLIER**

Illustrations © 2005 by Bryan Collier.
Reprinted by permission of Henry Holt Books
for Young Readers. All Rights Reserved.

2017 WINNER

Radiant Child: The Story of Young Artist Jean-Michel Basquiat, **JAVAKA STEPTOE**

Used courtesy of Little, Brown Books for Young Readers.

1993 WINNER

The Origin of Life on Earth: An African Creation Myth, **KATHLEEN ATKINS WILSON**

The Origin of Life on Earth: An African Creation Myth, by David A. Anderson,
illustrated by Kathleen Atkins Wilson (Sights Productions, LLC, 1991).

1992 WINNER

Tar Beach, **FAITH RINGGOLD**

Illustrations from *Tar Beach* by Faith Ringgold. © 1991 by Faith Ringgold. Used by permission of Crown Publishers, an imprint of Random House Children's Books, a division of Penguin Random House LLC. All rights reserved.

2008 WINNER

Let It Shine: Three Favorite Spirituals, **ASHLEY BRYAN**

Illustration © 2007 by Ashley Bryan from *Let It Shine: Three Favorite Spirituals* published by Atheneum Books for Young Readers, an imprint of Simon & Schuster Children's Publishing. Used with permission of the publisher.

2002 WINNER

Goin' Someplace Special, **JERRY PINKNEY**

Illustration © 2001 by Jerry Pinkney from *Goin' Someplace Special* written by Patricia C. McKissack, published by Simon & Schuster Books for Young Readers, an imprint of Simon & Schuster Children's Publishing. Used with permission of the publisher.

1998 WINNER

In Daddy's Arms I Am Tall: African Americans Celebrating Fathers, **JAVAKA STEPTOE**

1994 WINNER

Soul Looks Back in Wonder, **TOM FEELINGS**

2001 WINNER
Uptown, **BRYAN COLLIER**

Illustrations © 2000 by Bryan Collier. Reprinted by permission
of Henry Holt Books for Young Readers. All Rights Reserved.

2018 WINNER
Out of Wonder: Poems Celebrating Poets, **EKUA HOLMES**

Illustrations © 2017 by Ekua Holmes. Reproduced by permission
of the publisher, Candlewick Press, Somerville, Massachusetts.

2003 WINNER

Talkin' About Bessie: The Story of Aviator Elizabeth Coleman, **E. B. LEWIS**

Reprinted by permission of Scholastic Inc.

1995 WINNER

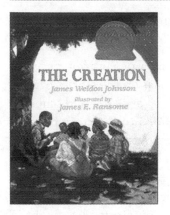

JOHNSON, JAMES WELDON. *The Creation.* Illustrated by James E. Ransome. Holiday House, 1994. Gr. K–3.

A tribute to the ageless quality of James Weldon Johnson's poetic narration of the creation of the world is captured in a dramatic contemporary setting especially appropriate for today's youth. James Ransome, reflecting the power of oral tradition, portrays a wise and warm storyteller sharing the events with a rapt audience of young people. The illustrator gives life to the stirring words with tones of color and a use of perspective that interprets the vastness of God's world and the move from emptiness to inhabitation. The lyrical beauty of the words is enhanced by the surrounding borders that depict the step-by-step development of the sermon until the dramatic moment when "man became a living soul" whose very physique exudes strength and purpose.

1995 HONORS

GRIMES, NIKKI. *Meet Danitra Brown.* Illustrated by Floyd Cooper. Lothrop, Lee, & Shepard, 1994. Gr. 3–5.

Danitra Brown is an exuberant, spunky, self-assured young person. Through Nikki Grimes's poetry, Danitra expresses her "philosophy" on the importance of exposure to things of culture, how to react to those who try to "put you down," the beauty of Blackness, and other important facts of life. Floyd Cooper's illustrations capture Danitra's energy in images of her often leaping into the air, engaging in spirited dancing, and, in pensive moments, with a sense of life and well being in her sparkling eyes shining through black-rimmed glasses. Cooper consistently dresses Danitra in tones of her favorite color—purple—sometimes stripes, sometimes plaids, sometimes plain, but always purple. The illustrator symbolically uses muted tones of brown for the background as well as for the skin tones of the characters in the poetry. The words and pictures reveal Danitra Brown through wise and joyful animation—"the greatest and most splendiferous girl in town."

MEDEARIS, ANGELA SHELF. *The Singing Man.* Illustrated by Terea Shaffer. Holiday House, 1994. Gr. 3–5.

The Singing Man is a folktale that lauds the importance of the griot, or praise singer, whose responsibility it is to preserve and pass on the stories of Africa's glorious history—the achievements of its rulers, artisans, and scholars. Terea Shaffer's rich oil paintings not only add drama to the story but also give visualization to the diversity of the people in Nigerian regions as readers travel with the praise singer, Banzar, and his teacher Sholo. The sun-baked lands over which they travel, the variations in clothing design, the facial features that distinguish one group of people from another, and the musical instruments that were used to tell the griot's stories are caught in the expressive, informative illustrations that give life to an age-old tale.

1994 WINNER

FEELINGS, TOM. *Soul Looks Back in Wonder.* Dial, 1993. Gr. 3–5.

To convey the joy, beauty, and challenge of being African American, Tom Feelings invited African American poets to contribute original poems to accompany his paintings. A never-before-published poem by Langston Hughes is also included. Using a variety of techniques and mixed media, such as collage, color crayon, and wallpaper, Feelings has created a book that is captivating to the eye and musical to those who listen. The artist offers striking images of copper-colored boys and girls, children with beautiful dark faces—the youth this book was designed to inspire. In this, the artist's first book done in color throughout, the predominant colors are the blended and textured blues, greens, and browns of Feelings's beloved Mother Africa. Brief biographical sketches of each of the contributing poets are included.

1994 HONORS

THOMAS, JOYCE CAROL. *Brown Honey in Broomwheat Tea.* **Illustrated by** Floyd Cooper. HarperCollins, 1993. Gr. 3–5.

The striking paintings of African Americans in *Brown Honey in Broomwheat Tea* give dramatic visualization to Joyce Carol Thomas's provocative poetry. Stirring examples of this visual feast can be seen in the strength and dignity of the white-haired elder's face when sipping broomwheat tea, in the artist's interpretation of the African American lineage as generations rise from the interwoven roots of a sturdy tree, and in the trusting face of the child who asks that "as you would cherish a thing of beauty, cherish me."

A touch of sunshine yellow illuminates some part of each page—symbolic of the light of hope that is the strength of the African American race. Cooper's art reveals a sensitivity to Thomas's words, resulting in a book that in word and picture is a celebration of African American life.

MITCHELL, MARGAREE KING. *Uncle Jed's Barbershop.* **Illustrated by** James E. Ransome. Simon & Schuster, 1993. Gr. 3–5.

Set in the rural South, *Uncle Jed's Barbershop* is a story about holding fast to a dream in spite of seemingly overwhelming obstacles. Uncle Jed's goal in life was to own his own barbershop with four chairs, mirrors, sinks with running water, and a red-and-white barber pole on the outside. Beset by the Depression, bank failures, and prejudice, Uncle Jed is forced to defer his dream. Finally, at age seventy-nine, he opens his barbershop to the delight of all who were his "customers" over the years.

James Ransome's paintings, full of vibrant colors, capture the moods and extend the text of Mitchell's story. Uncle Jed is a sturdy man, cheerful and undefeated. One can observe the artist's attention to historical accuracy in the paintings of the potbellied stove, the crystal-set radio, the oval rag rug—all typical of the era in which the story is set. The furniture, the oval mirrors in the barbershop, and even the broom as he sweeps up at the end of the day impart emotions of the joy of ownership.

1993 WINNER

ANDERSON, DAVID A. *The Origin of Life on Earth: An African Creation Myth.* Illustrated by Kathleen Atkins Wilson. Sights, 1991. Gr. K–5.

The Origin of Life on Earth is a Yoruba legend of how the world began. Kathleen Atkins Wilson saw in the story a moving part of her own heritage. With breathtaking skill, she used her distinctive style of portraying "silhouette expressions of portraits in black" to translate the story into a visual "telling." As the Coretta Scott King awards jury looked at this book, they felt wonderment at how many details of the text were expanded in the illustrations. There was the care of detailing the stages in the molding of each figure and the quiet respect for the shapes of the disabled—representing the orisha Obatala's moment of drunken weakness. And what a contrast between the distinctive and expressive features of the silhouetted story characters and the luminous clothing in which they are garbed! Wilson's unique artistic style gives unforgettable life to a well-told story that shouts her joy and pride in her African heritage.

1993 HONORS

WILLIAMS, SHERLEY ANNE. *Working Cotton.* Illustrated by Carole Byard. Harcourt Brace Jovanovich, 1992. Gr. Pre-K–3.

Double-page spreads illustrated in acrylics with mottled hues set the mood in this powerful visual rendition of a day in the life of a Black migrant family. As the day unfolds through the voice and eyes of young Shelan, Byard depicts the strength of this family through large close-up images and lush colors. The beauty of the illustrations never softens the powerful images of work and struggle that are conveyed in the text. We see the immensity of the cotton fields and the strain of hard work, yet the tenderness of the expressions reminds us of the power of love and family as the summer heat heightens weariness. It is a celebration of strength in an unjust world that makes such strength necessary to survive.

WAHL, JAN. *Little Eight John.* **Illustrated by Wil Clay.** Lodestar, 1992. Gr. K–2.

Little Eight John, a familiar character in African American folklore, is an extremely handsome young fellow but just as naughty as he is good looking. Wil Clay has captured every nuance of this mischievous child's behavior in what seem like double-vision settings. When the text speaks of one of Eight John's tricks, which causes his mother to have the hiccups, the illustration creates an illusion of movement similar to seasickness. When Eight John is admonished not to sit backward in a chair, the chair suddenly becomes a horse being whipped into frenzied action by the overactive boy. Wahl's adaptation of this popular story has a happy ending, which Clay captures in the affectionate scene between a relieved mother and a repentant Little Eight John. For a visual treat, readers will enjoy examining each picture for the details that tell so much more of the story.

SAN SOUCI, ROBERT. *Sukey and the Mermaid.* **Illustrated by Brian Pinkney.** Four Winds, 1992. Gr. 3–5.

With his scratchboard technique, Brian Pinkney has captured many subtle nuances that give an added dimension to San Souci's interpretation of this tale from the folklore of South Carolina. Using gentle touches of color, Pinkney brings the figures to life in true character—the darkness of the evil father, the emerald sea colors of the mermaid, and the childlike pink in the clothing of the beleaguered young Sukey, who is abused by her greedy father. A closer look shows that the artist is also attentive to such tiny details as the part in Sukey's hair or the wisps of smoke from the father's pipe. The skillful blend of words and pictures assures the reader that *Sukey and the Mermaid* is a story to be read, to be told, and to be looked at over and over.

1992 WINNER

RINGGOLD, FAITH. *Tar Beach.* Crown, 1991. Gr. K–3.

Faith Ringgold is an artist and a quilter. With creative ingenuity, Ringgold weaves a story of hope, dreams, and dauntless courage stitched with the innocence of childhood. The reader meets Cassie Louise Lightfoot as she spends a hot summer evening on the roof of the apartment house—

the city child's "tar beach." Looking at the sky, Cassie flies over a world in which her talented father will be able to work on tall buildings because, even though he is Black, he will be able to join the union. She sees her family with enough income so that her hardworking mother will be able to sleep late some mornings. Then, Cassie dreams of having ice cream for dessert every night because she will own the Ice Cream Factory. On all her imaginary travels, she takes her little brother BeBe and all who read this thoughtful picture book. The choice of colors and patterns for the material in the *Tar Beach* quilt and the arrangement of figures in the various scenes offer both a feast for the eye and food for thought.

1992 HONORS

BRYAN, ASHLEY. *All Night, All Day: A Child's First Book of African-American Spirituals*. Atheneum, 1991. Gr. Pre-K–5.

More than once Ashley Bryan has voiced his concern that young African Americans and other youth are not being exposed to the melodic beauty and the historical significance of Negro spirituals. *All Night, All Day* is one of several books that this artist and scholar has designed to make the words and the music of the spirituals accessible and aesthetically pleasing to young audiences.

Bryan uses tints and shades of tempera colors to illustrate the changing moods of the twenty titles included in this collection. Bright yellow glimmers in the abstract candles in "This Little Light of Mine," and swirling blues and sea greens wash around brown-hued feet in "Wade in the Water." And one cannot miss the joyous, repetitious, double-page spread of the huge bells accompanying the spiritual "Peter, Go Ring the Bells."

At the 1992 Coretta Scott King Book Awards breakfast there was an unforgettable moment of silence when, as his acceptance "speech" for this honor book, Ashley Bryan played the title piece, "All Night, All Day," on his recorder. Bryan has given us a book and an experience to be remembered for many nights and many days.

GREENFIELD, ELOISE. *Night on Neighborhood Street*. Illustrated by Jan Spivey Gilchrist. Dial, 1991. Gr. K–3.

Jan Spivey Gilchrist's use of soft shading together with blue, gold, and green illustrates the characters portrayed in Eloise Greenfield's poetry. The expressions on the faces of the children and adults and the subtle use of body language complement the author's poetry. The artist's use of silhouette and shadings of black and white intensify the visual impact. Given that the passage of time plays a strong role in the book, Gilchrist's use of light and shadow and such details as curtains blowing as night approaches set a mood and enhance the overall effect.

Communication between writer and artist can be seen in how the words and the pictures evoke visual images that change with each poem. The children's faces show adoration, mischievousness, apprehension, fear, sadness, or grief as called for by the corresponding poems. The adults, even when captured only in shadow or silhouette, convey movement and emotion. A fine example of this is the piece "In the Church." The interaction between children and adults is well presented in such pieces as "Goodnight Juma," "Fambly Time," and "The Seller." *Night on Neighborhood Street* is a magnificent creation of mystical appearances through the use of color, light, and shading.

1991 WINNER

PRICE, LEONTYNE, ADAPT. *Aïda.* Illustrated by Leo Dillon and Diane Dillon. Harcourt Brace Jovanovich, 1990. Gr. 3–8.

Leo and Diane Dillon, inspired by the voice of Leontyne Price singing the title role of *Aïda,* knew that the diva's adaptation of this tragic opera demanded artistic interpretation. Each bordered, full-page illustration reveals some aspect of a palace of ancient Egypt. The artists' dedication to honesty in the portrayal of the characters, their clothing, the setting in which they functioned, and the grandeur of the period is clearly visible. The Dillons capture the individuality of each character in the huge cast of this tragic drama. The Dillons's creativity extends to the friezes across the top of the page—a pageant of Egyptian personages adds to the visualization of the text. The depth of the Dillons's research reflects their commitment to providing an accurate picture of the dignity of an ancient and learned people. Aïda is a story of warring factions, unrequited love, and, finally, the fatal price of loyalty.

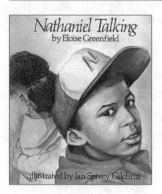

1990 WINNER

GREENFIELD, ELOISE. *Nathaniel Talking.* Illustrated by Jan Spivey Gilchrist. Black Butterfly Children's Books, 1988. Gr. K–5.

Jan Spivey Gilchrist uses only black-and-white pencil sketches to portray a wide range of emotions—sadness, grief, joy, pensiveness—that are the themes of some of Eloise Greenfield's poems. In "My Daddy," Nathaniel's face shows us he is completely at one with his father's music and secure in his father's love for him. Nathaniel says, "He ain't never been on TV, but to me he's a big star." There is sadness in Nathaniel's face as he sits in his room, thinking about his mama, who died last year. But one perceives a source of comfort in the shadowed figure of the father entering his son's room. Pictures in close harmony with the words demonstrate the artist's sensitivity as she depicts events in the life of the spunky Nathaniel and his friends. Gilchrist clearly understands all the nuances in Greenfield's poetry and interprets the poems with clarity and a warmness of spirit.

1990 HONOR

SAN SOUCI, ROBERT D., RETELLER. *The Talking Eggs.* Illustrated by Jerry Pinkney. Dial, 1989. Gr. K–5.

A Creole folktale from the southern U.S. oral tradition, *The Talking Eggs* features two sisters: a favored, spoiled, and lazy girl named Rose and a generous, kind, and a hard-working girl named Blanche. The girls are given identical tasks by a mysterious woman in the woods, and Blanche is rewarded for her trust and obedience. This beautifully designed and printed version of a folktale previously known to many in its Anglo-European variant features African American characters wonderfully realized by Jerry Pinkney. His drawing and painting show fresh observations of people and of the animal world. They embody a richness of detail and motion that is harmonious with the tale's idiom, time, and place. In addition to being a Coretta Scott King honor book, *The Talking Eggs* was a Caldecott honor book.

1989 WINNER

MCKISSACK, PATRICIA C. *Mirandy and Brother Wind.* **Illustrated by Jerry Pinkney.** Knopf, 1988. Gr. K–5.

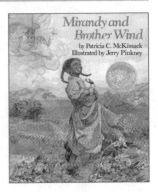

Mirandy overlooks her obvious partner for her first cakewalk after she brags that she will be accompanied by the wind himself and sets out to catch her partner. The engaging full-color paintings are filled with historical details of African American life in the rural South at the turn of the century. They perfectly interpret and enhance the light-hearted exuberance inherent in the story and memorably characterize the pride, self-confidence, and determination of Mirandy.

1989 HONORS

STOLZ, MARY. *Storm in the Night.* **Illustrated by Pat Cummings.** Harper & Row, 1988. Gr. Pre-K–3.

Grandfather's lively recollection about his own childhood fear of a thunderstorm occupies young Thomas's attention during an electrical power failure and helps the boy overcome his worries. A visual story-within-a-story assists readers with the flashbacks. Cummings's ability to challenge the eye with color and perspective is as effective as her poignant portrayal of the African American grandfather and grandson inside their cozy single-family home on a rainy summer night.

GREENFIELD, ELOISE. *Under the Sunday Tree.* **Illustrated by Mr. Amos Ferguson.** Harper & Row, 1988. Gr. K–6.

Twenty exquisite paintings introduce children to the artwork of the Bahamian artist Mr. Amos Ferguson. The playfully vivid paintings, which boldly depict aspects of life in the Bahamas, have great child appeal. Poet Eloise Greenfield has written poems to accompany every painting, further extending each painting's mood and meaning.

1988 WINNER

STEPTOE, JOHN. *Mufaro's Beautiful Daughters: An African Tale.* Lothrop, Lee, & Shepard, 1987. Gr. K–5.

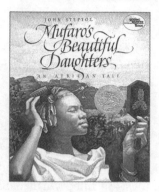

Two beautiful sisters—one vain, the other kind—compete for the king's attention when he announces he is looking for a wife. Brilliant full-color paintings illustrate the classic tale of just rewards. The artist skillfully uses light and color to give emotional power to illustrations that richly detail the natural beauty of a specific region in Zimbabwe.

1988 HONORS

LANGSTAFF, JOHN, COMPOSER. *What a Morning! The Christmas Story in Black Spirituals.* Illustrated by **Ashley Bryan.** Margaret K. McElderry, 1987. Gr. K–6.

The Christmas story is told through a chronological arrangement of five African American spirituals, lavishly illustrated by brilliant tempera paintings. Brief biblical quotes accompanying each of the spirituals provide a religious context, while Bryan's shining iconographic portraits of a Black Nativity provide a historical, geographical, and emotional context.

ROHMER, HARRIET, OCTAVIO CHOW, AND MORRIS VIDAURE. *The Invisible Hunters: A Legend from the Miskito Indians of Nicaragua / Los Cazadores Invisibles: Una Leyenda de los Indios Miskitos de Nicaragua.* Illustrated by **Joe Sam.** Children's Book Press, 1987.

An early Central American legend tells of the ultimate price of greed as well as the tragedy of deceiving one's own people. Themes concerning colonialism are developed in colorful, unique paper constructions and collages.

1987 WINNER

DRAGONWAGON, CRESCENT. *Half a Moon and One Whole Star.* **Illustrated by Jerry Pinkney.** Macmillan, 1986. Gr. Pre-K–3.

Half a Moon and One Whole Star is a lullaby that invites the reader to share in the safety of untroubled sleep. It is the song of man and of creature and their different activities as the sun goes down. It is as if Pinkney were an unseen observer in the actions of each character in this gentle story. One sees the brightly colored parrots "rest in jungles deep." And at the same time Pinkney takes the reader with him to see "Johnny with his saxophone" standing against an early night sky, Johnny who will play at the club at night. And while the activities are either stopping or starting, with mood-setting colors the illustrator introduces the reader to the child who at the end of the day is lulled to untroubled sleep. In a blend of words and pictures, the reader, too, can sing of the night that is marked with *Half a Moon and One Whole Star.*

1987 HONORS

BRYAN, ASHLEY. *Lion and the Ostrich Chicks: And Other African Folk Tales.* Atheneum, 1986. Gr. K–6.

Using his special talent for blending rhythmic word patterns with all the details of a well-told story, Bryan has adapted a diverse collection of African tales that beg to be read aloud. Through his research into the history and culture of several tribes, this author-illustrator found the roots of the stories in many geographical regions and, in his inimitable writing style, retold the tales for young readers. Complete scholar that he is, Bryan has included a bibliography listing his sources for all the stories in the book.

One cannot miss the folktale concept of the triumph of good over evil, whether it is in the title story, in which the lion tries to claim the ostrich chicks as his own, or in a telling of how the born-foolish boy outwits the trickster Ananse.

Bryan extends the text with his own art prints in sharp black-and-white figures or in illustrations using the earth colors of the land in which the tales are set. The Coretta Scott King awards jury enjoyed both the humor and the lessons in *Lion and the Ostrich Chicks*.

CUMMINGS, PAT. *C.L.O.U.D.S.* Lothrop, Lee, & Shepard, 1986. Gr. 3–5.

In a flight of fancy, Cummings lets readers share in an imaginary trip to an artist's studio where the painter hopes to see exciting new colors spring from his palette. Chuku is a painter for Creative Lights Opticals and Unusual Designs in the Sky. His excitement about a new assignment fades when he is sent to paint the sky over New York City and to produce rigid and realistic interpretations. But his creativity is not to be thwarted. Each day he draws sky pictures in unusual colors and intriguing cloud shapes. There are Lovely Light Lavender sunsets, Cloud-Lining Silver, and Unbelievingly Brilliant Gold. The clouds take the shapes of tigers, giraffes, and birds, all of which are done especially for a little girl, Chrissy, the only one in New York who ever seems to look up.

But all readers who see Chuku's figures in *C.L.O.U.D.S.* will find themselves looking for colorful skies in New York and elsewhere. They may even look for a real Chuku, who is a very purple young man.

1986 WINNER

FLOURNOY, VALERIE. *The Patchwork Quilt.* Illustrated by Jerry Pinkney. Dial, 1985. Gr. Pre-K–3.

The Patchwork Quilt is a story of family unity. In this story, parents care, children are loved, and a grandmother is a loving and integral part of the household. Each member of the family contributes a memorable piece of clothing to the patchwork quilt, which symbolically bonds the family. Jerry Pinkney saw all these elements in the text and gave his personal artistic interpretation to the story and its characters. In the colorful quilt, one sees a variety of textures, shapes, and forms. This same concept extends itself to the characterization of the family members. Pinkney captures the nuances of skin color, the individual hairstyles, and the personal choices of dress. This care for making each character an individual speaks to the artist's philosophy of making sure those who see his art realize that the beauty of the African American is as varied as the people who make up this culture. The artwork in *The Patchwork Quilt* invites readers to visit a cross-generational African American family living in harmony in a home that celebrates togetherness.

1986 HONOR

HAMILTON, VIRGINIA. *The People Could Fly: American Black Folktales.*
Illustrated by Leo Dillon and Diane Dillon. Knopf, 1985. Gr. 3–6.

Forty stunning, stylized, black-and-white illustrations accompany Virginia Hamilton's retellings of African American folktales, echoing the dignity of the text by extending each tale's distinctive mood. The harmony of all book-design elements provides a handsome presentation of stories for families to share, scholars to study, and individuals of all ages and backgrounds to enjoy.

1984 WINNER

WALTER, MILDRED PITTS. *My Mama Needs Me.*
Illustrated by Pat Cummings. Lothrop, Lee, & Shepard, 1983. Gr. K–2.

Walter's simple text describes a universal dilemma—the concern and discomfort of the older child when a new baby comes home—and Cummings gives visual interpretation to the concept. She chooses mainly mocha brown for the family figures and uses other colors to give the story a multicultural setting, thus extending the universality of the concept. An outstanding feature of the illustrations can be seen in the expressive eyes of the troubled Jason—eyes that show the perplexity of wanting to be needed yet seeming to be rejected. There is a visual sense of family, of love and tenderness, when Jason shares the mother's nursing moments and learns to rub the baby's ear to make it want to suckle more, and when he is asked to help bathe the baby. From Jason's feelings of being an outsider to the assurance that his mama needs him, Cummings's bright colors and decorative designs capture the joy of this family story.

1983 WINNER

MAGUBANE, PETER. *Black Child.* Knopf, 1982.
Gr. 6–12*

Taking advantage of the sharp contrasts that are best captured in black-and-white photography, photojournalist Magubane has shown the disparate worlds of South Africa through the eyes of its Black children. The pictures tell stories of the deplorable working conditions of teenagers who should be enjoying life but are instead sweating in the maize fields of Delmas and who return at day's end to windowless dormitories for restless sleep. As a tribute to the human spirit, Magubane photographed a youth making joyful music on a homemade guitar. The book closes with a dramatic picture of the grave of Hector Peterson—the thirteen-year-old who was the first to die in the Soweto riots.

There seems to be a special message in the selection of the solid black endpapers with which this powerful photo documentary opens and closes.

1983 HONORS

BRYAN, ASHLEY, SELECTOR AND ILLUSTRATOR. *I'm Going to Sing: Black American Spirituals. v. 2.* Atheneum, 1982. Gr. K–12.

Bryan has spent many hours in the research of African American history in subject areas from folklore and legend to poetry and music. With a concern for making spirituals accessible and meaningful to young people, he designed and illustrated his second volume of those songs using woodblock images reflecting the "spirit of the early religious woodblock books." With special skill, Bryan depicts facial expressions and body movements that reflect the moods of the songs—which range from hopeful, to longing, to joyful and triumphant. In what the artist describes as a desire for visual unity, with a technique that must have required unbelievable patience, he carved the notes using the same woodblock style as the illustrations. The Coretta Scott King awards jury was impressed not only with the words and music but also with the fact that the notes all had to be cut in reverse so that they would print out correctly. In selecting this title for illustration honors, the committee agreed that now more young people were surely going to sing.

CAINES, JEANNETTE. *Just Us Women.* Illustrated by Pat Cummings. Harper & Row, 1982. Gr. K–3.

The text is simple and very positively feminine. Aunt Martha is taking her young niece to North Carolina in her new convertible. The trip is to be made with "No boys and no men, just us women." Cummings captures the joy of the trip in two-tone color illustrations that extend the text. One sees a small picture of shoe boxes overflowing with lunch goodies; a double spread shows the fun of roadside shopping; a background of moon and stars completes the picture when the travelers decide to have breakfast at night. The warmth of companionship is undeniable when at the end of the trip, the two "women," with arms around each other, approach the relatives' home at the end of a joyous journey. *Just Us Women* is a rich and positive concept interpreted with artistic skill.

ADOFF, ARNOLD. *All the Colors of the Race.* Illustrated by John Steptoe. Lothrop, Lee, & Shepard, 1982. Gr. 5–12.

Distinguished brown-tone paintings provide the perfect accompaniment to Adoff's free-form poems written from the point of view of a girl born to parents of different ethnic backgrounds—one white, one African American. Steptoe's expressionistic portraits capture the many moods of a young girl searching for identity, respect, and security as she struggles to assert herself in a sometimes hostile world.

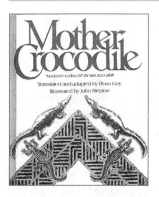

1982 WINNER

DIOP, BIRAGO. TRANS. AND ADAPTED BY ROSA GUY. *Mother Crocodile / Maman-Caiman.* Illustrated by John Steptoe. Delacorte, 1981. (New edition: *Mother Crocodile: An Uncle Amadou Tale from Senegal.* Delacorte, 1982.) Gr. K–3.

When Mother Crocodile warns her children to swim away, they close their ears. Only later, when it's almost too late, do they realize the truth in her words. Steptoe's breathtaking abstract illustrations are appropriately presented in a spectrum of underwater colors to create a strong sense of place while at the same time allowing for interpretation of symbolic history in this cautionary Ovolof tale from West Africa.

1982 HONOR

GREENFIELD, ELOISE. *Daydreamers.* Illustrated by Tom Feelings. Dial, 1981. Gr. K–5.

To read *Daydreamers,* one must first closely study the faces of the children brought sensitively to life by the artist Feelings. The figures of children outlined in chocolate brown, charcoal gray, and sepia convey determination, self-confidence, and a strong feeling that they are a part of the future. There is a message in the set of the jaw of some of the young men remembering their history and "drawing strength from the spirit of their ancestors."

Is it the placement of hand on hip that shouts, "I am somebody"? One wonders what thoughts are going through the mind of the toddler pensively sucking on a tiny finger. The eyes of some of the children—eyes looking into the future—seem to reflect Greenfield's words, "daydreamers letting the world dizzy itself without them." From toddler to young adult, the characters in Feelings's illustrations proclaim that "dreaming has made them new."

Feelings's illustrations have more than an aesthetic impact. There is a message of ethnic pride and cultural strength that is totally integrated with Greenfield's poetic text.

1981 WINNER

BRYAN, ASHLEY. *Beat the Story-Drum, Pum-Pum.* Atheneum, 1980. Gr. 3–5.

The striking force of Bryan's lusty woodcut technique had instant appeal to the Coretta Scott King awards jury that selected this collection of tales based on Nigerian folklore. There is a rhythm in the curve of the animals' bodies that captures the rollicking beat and humor of Bryan's storytelling. Subtle use of lines gives expressions to the faces of the characters in the stories—stories that explain why the elephant and the bush cow do not get along or that take a jab at human foibles as in the tale of the man who could not keep a wife because he insisted on counting each spoonful of food placed on his plate.

Reflecting Bryan's strong concern for truth, there is a consistency between the setting—the plains of Africa—and the choice of colors. This is particularly discernible in the full-page illustrations that show blends of earth tones—reds, browns, oranges—as one would see in the homeland of these stories.

1981 HONORS

GREENFIELD, ELOISE. *Grandma's Joy.* Illustrated by Carole Byard. Philomel, 1980. Gr. Pre-K–3.

Charcoal drawings on cream paper tenderly express Greenfield's story of Rhondy's attempts to cheer her grandmother, who is sadly packing their belongings into boxes as they prepare to move away. Remembering the special closeness they have shared since Rhondy was a little baby finally cheers and comforts Grandmama. The expressiveness of the illustrations brings an immediacy and a loving respect for people struggling against difficult times, pulling the reader into the story and championing the strength of family ties that carry us through. The illustrations honestly portray both the sadness of the story and the glow of joy and love that comforts child and adult.

ZASLAVSKY, CLAUDIA. *Count on Your Fingers African Style.* Illustrated by Jerry Pinkney. Crowell, 1980. Gr. K–3.

In an African marketplace, young readers are introduced to a way of counting based on the system used in some areas of that vast continent. Pinkney gives graphic life to the concept through clear, black-and-white illustrations. Even without color one can clearly visualize the marketplace and sense its busyness. And indeed the absence of color makes very clear the position of the fingers and the movements of the hands that distinguish one number from another. The uncluttered illustrations in this book serve as a fun-filled, participatory introduction to an element of mathematics in another language.

1980 WINNER

YARBROUGH, CAMILLE. *Cornrows.*
Illustrated by Carole Byard. Coward, McCann,
& Geoghegan, 1979. Gr. 3–6.

As a modern-day grandmother and mama braid their children's hair in cornrows, the three generations share the stories of the braid patterns that are a part of their African heritage. The charcoal drawings with swirling shapes and dramatic close-ups present a series of visions, first taking the reader to Africa and then offering a series of distinct portraits of famous Black Americans. Shifting from masks and drums to Malcolm X and Rosa Parks, the drawings soften or become crisp as appropriate. The illustrations of African carvings impart solidity, while the drawings depicting the joy of dancing flutter with movement. In the series of portraits of leaders and heroes of Black America, each person is easily recognizable and aptly presented. Included are Langston Hughes, Malcolm X, and Marian Anderson. There are no stilted copies of studio portraits here but instead vivid people joyously and proudly leading their kin—people like the three generations of family glorying in their heritage, in the ordinary world of home, storytelling, and braiding cornrows.

1979 WINNER

GRIMES, NIKKI. *Something on My Mind.*
Illustrated by Tom Feelings. Dial, 1978. Gr. 4–8.

Tom Feelings captures the essence of Nikki Grimes's words in the faces and body language of the inner-city children of whom she writes. The words are often poignant, speaking of the need to belong, the wish to understand "the secrets grown-ups share," or just to understand grown-ups. Feelings's charcoal and sepia drawings leave no doubt about the message of each piece. There is quiet puzzlement on the face of the young lady, for example, who tries to understand the dichotomy of the mother who urges her to hurry into her Sunday best to go to the Lord's house and then emits some telling curses when she bangs her toe. "Why," asks the child, "instead of going to the Lord's house, don't we invite him to visit ours?" Feelings's line drawings are deceptively simple. The beauty of African American features shows in the face of each child portrayed in this thought-provoking collection.

1978 WINNER

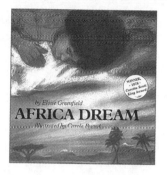

GREENFIELD, ELOISE. *Africa Dream.* Illustrated by Carole Byard. John Day, 1977. Gr. K–2.

In a dream sequence, a huge, crashing wave transports a sleeping child from her home in one land to her homeland in Africa. Together, the girl and the reader celebrate the wonders of her heritage—magnificent examples of majestic buildings, the sounds of drums and song, a glimpse of everyday activities, and the powerful strength of noble ancestors welcoming her home. The varying shades of charcoal used throughout seem to symbolize a time past. The creative use of dimension conveys the dramatic contrast between the leaders of old and the little figure to whom welcoming arms are extended. *Africa Dream,* and the story it tells, is deceptively simple in word and picture.

1974 WINNER

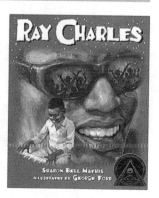

MATHIS, SHARON BELL. *Ray Charles.* Illustrated by George Ford. Crowell, 1973. Gr. 3–6*

When Ford did the illustrations for Mathis's *Ray Charles,* little did he know that he would become a part of history! Indeed, the drawings in this young readers' biography made Ford the very first illustrator to receive the coveted Coretta Scott King Book Award plaque and an honorarium.

Ford expresses the joy of Ray Charles's music beginning with the very cover picture—a smiling musician with swaying dancers reflected in his dark glasses. Looking at black-and-white sketches interspersed with yellow-toned figures, one can follow the talented pianist from his early days, when he lost his sight, through the school where he learned to write down his own musical notations and on to scenes of large audiences enjoying the sounds of spirituals, blues, and jazz.

CONTRIBUTORS

CONTRIBUTORS TO THE CURRENT EDITION

Rudine Sims Bishop
Sam Bloom
Jessica Anne Bratt
Irene Briggs
Miriam Lang Budin
Patty Carleton
Kathy Caroll
LaKeshia N. Darden
Omobolade Delano-
  Oriarian, PhD
Christina Dorr

Jason Driver
Carol Edwards
Suzanne Fondrie, PhD
Sujin Huggins
Chrystal Carr Jeter
Sharon Levin
Erica Marks
Veronica Muniz-Soto
Laverne Page
Linda M. Pavonetti,
  PhD, Ed.D

Sandra Payne
Marguerite W. Penick-
  Parks, PhD
Susan Polos
April Roy
Nichole Shabazz
Barbara Spears
Ida W. Thompson
Christina Vortia
Bina Williams

CONTRIBUTORS TO PREVIOUS EDITIONS

Lana Adlawan
Eunice Anderson
Rita Auerbach
Therese Bigelow
Rudine Sims Bishop
Lesley Colabucci
Eboni Curry
Rose Timmons Dawson
Dr. Cora Phelps Dunkley
Carol Edwards

Dorothy Evans
Diane Foote
Debra Gold
Darwin Henderson, EdD
Kathleen Horning
Hilda Weeks Kuter
Karen Lemmons
Carole J. McCollough,
  PhD
Ann Miller

Susan Pines
Adelaide Poniatowski
  Phelps
Martha Ruff
Sue Sherif
Henrietta M. Smith
Robin Smith
Deborah D. Taylor

SUBJECT INDEX

FAMILY STORIES

FANNIE LOU HAMER

INDEX